24th Marathon des Sables

24TH MARATHON DES SABLES

A COMPETITOR'S TALE

STEVE CUSHING

Copyright © 2010 Steve Cushing

The moral right of the author has been asserted.

Apart from any fair dealing for the purposes of research or private study, or criticism or review, as permitted under the Copyright, Designs and Patents Act 1988, this publication may only be reproduced, stored or transmitted, in any form or by any means, with the prior permission in writing of the publishers, or in the case of reprographic reproduction in accordance with the terms of licences issued by the Copyright Licensing Agency. Enquiries concerning reproduction outside those terms should be sent to the publishers.

Matador
5 Weir Road
Kibworth Beauchamp
Leicester LE8 0LQ, UK
Tel: (+44) 116 279 2277
Email: books@troubador.co.uk
Web: www.troubador.co.uk/matador

ISBN 978 1848762 862

British Library Cataloguing in Publication Data.
A catalogue record for this book is available from the British Library.

Typeset in 11pt Book Sabon by Troubador Publishing Ltd, Leicester, UK
Printed in Great Britain by the MPG Books Group, Bodmin and King's Lynn

Matador is an imprint of Troubador Publishing Ltd

Dedicated to

Cherith

*My constant support over the three years of my amazing journey.
I could not have done it without you.*

Alistair, Jenny and Nicola

I am so proud of what you are all achieving. I hope what you read inspires you to reach your own maximum potential

Tent 95

It was a privilege to share a tent with Ant Riley, Joe Skinner, Martin Hallworth, Nick Zambelis, Richard Webster, Rob Jackson and Russell Muldoon

1 tent, 8 strong individuals, 1 great team

CONTENTS

Introduction		ix
Section One	The Marathon des Sables, Morocco and the Sahara Desert	1
1.	The Marathon des Sables	3
2.	Morocco and the Sahara Desert	14
Section Two	My Training	19
3.	Initial training and moving to ultra marathons	21
4.	Training – Phase 2 – Upping the Tempo	32
5.	Training – Phase 3 – Back to Back Sessions	40
6.	Training – Phase 4 – Tapering and the Heat Chamber	51
Section Three	Planning and Preparation	57
7.	Essential equipment, Medical kit and Hygiene	59
8.	Shoes, Socks and Gaiters	67
9.	Running in the Nude – Just Sunglasses	75
10.	Food, Cooking and Salt Tablets	79
11.	Luxury Items and Packing	84
Section Four	The Bivouac, The Organisation and Tent 95	87
12.	The Bivouac, The Organisation and Tent 95	89
Section Five	My Diary	97
13.	Off to Morocco and Sahara Desert Storms	99

14.	Stage 1 Erg Chebbi to Erg Znaigui 19.5 miles	109
15.	Stage 2 Erg Znaigui - 22 miles	113
16.	Stage 3 Erg Znaigui to Aferdou Nsooualhine 57 miles	117
17.	Stage 4 Aferdou Nsooualhine to Tizinighrs 26.2 miles	131
18.	Return to Normality – in Stages	137
19.	The Road Maps	143

Section Six My Chosen Charity, The Happy House Project,
The Children of Watamu 149
20. Raising Money for Charity 151

Appendices		157
1.	Final Kit List / Food	158
2	Tent 95 Results	162

INTRODUCTION

On the 20th April 2006 I wrote a cheque for £500 as a deposit to enter the 23rd Marathon des Sables. I had recently returned from the Inaugural Antarctic Ice Marathon. It is often said that after such an event, and such an overwhelming experience, there is a period when you feel flat and even depressed. I do not recall my state of mind as I wrote the cheque, although some would argue it must have been unbalanced. I do know, however, that I had had an unforgettable experience running a marathon in the Antarctic Circle and I wanted to take on another challenge.

I had in fact first considered the Marathon des Sables almost 20 years before shortly after running my third marathon, in London, in a time of 3 hours and 18 minutes. A horse riding accident, in which I broke my pelvis in four places, put paid to that thought and any possibility once I recovered was abolished due to the responsibilities of a family of three children and a busy professional role as a single handed general medical practitioner, combined with an unsympathetic bank manager.

My entry to the Marathon des Sables was deferred until 2009 following a chance conversation with a friend and medical colleague, Mark Walker. At a party, which we both attended in July 2006, he mentioned to me that he would like to take part in the Marathon des Sables. I readily agreed to defer for a year with the possibility of running with him and one of his friends as a team. I understand that all places for the 24th Marathon des Sables were taken up within twelve minutes of the web site opening and Mark was not able to gain a place.

I had kept a diary when I was in Antarctica in 2006 and again when

I was husky dog sledding in the Arctic Circle in 2007. I have found this to be important as it is very easy to forget many of the details and the individual memories become a blur leaving only an overall impression and memory of the event. Being able to recall at a later date the individual memories, in my experience, enhances the total memory.

My tent mates noted my daily scribbling and encouraged me to write up my diary and to consider producing a book. This had never been my intention and my diary had been intended to be very much a personal record. I have, however, on reflection decided to take up their promptings and using my diary as the main section produce an individual competitors account of the 24th Marathon des Sables.

The information for this book, therefore, comes from a number of sources, none of which I had produced originally for the purpose for which they are now being used.

In Chapter 1 I have written a brief history of the Marathon des Sables to provide the background for what follows. I became aware while competing in this event that I knew nothing about the country in which I was living and so I have in Chapter 2 provided some information relating to Morocco, the Sahara Desert and the towns of Ouarzazete and Erfoud where we all spent some time.

I have outlined my training in Chapters 3 to 6. I had started writing a blog on 4th August 2008 which I attempted to update each week. The purpose of the blog had been to encourage sponsorship and was never intended to be converted into a chapter in a book. I have, however, used the information from my blog and have also used information from my very limited training diary (I must be one of the world's worst at completing such a diary) and from my Garmin watch which has a GPS system and records for each run my time, distance, elevation and heart rate. I have also used my blog, along with a probably flawed memory, to write chapters 7 to 11 which outline my planning for this event.

Chapter 12 introduces those individuals, who were to be so important in my time in the Sahara, my running companions in Tent 95. It also describes the bivouac and life in camp. My diary accompanied by some additional information which I have collated on my return is the source for chapters 13 to 19 which outline the days preceding the race, the race itself and the post race days. The diary was originally not intended for this purpose and so on the basis that "what goes on tour stays on tour" some sections have been omitted. (But Tent 95 will know why and for whom we were doing this event!)

Finally, although this is not a charity event, I along with many others, used the opportunity to raise money for charity. Chapter 20 describes my chosen charity, The Happy House Project for The Children of Watamu in Kenya.

The book is intended firstly for my wife and children and for future generations of the Cushing family. Secondly I hope it will provide permanent memories for all of us who shared six days in Tent 95. In addition it may be of interest to others who took part in the 24th Marathon des Sables and a source of interest and information for entrants to future episodes of this amazing event.

PART ONE

THE MARATHON DES SABLES

MOROCCO
AND
THE SAHARA DESERT

CHAPTER ONE

THE MARATHON DES SABLES

The Marathon des Sables is described as "the toughest footrace on earth". Whether or not it really deserves this recognition is open to debate. There are certainly races run over longer distances in very different conditions, such as the 6633 in the Arctic. This is a non-stop self sufficient race covering a distance of 350 miles, crossing the line of the Arctic Circle and continuing to the banks of the Arctic Ocean at Tuktoyaktuk. In similar vein is The Yukon Arctic Ultra covering 300 miles, with a 430 mile event held every two years. There are races which involve longer distances in one sustained effort than any of the stages of the Marathon des Sables such as Badwater, covering 135 miles non-stop from Death Valley to Mount Whitney, in temperatures up to 55 degrees C, with 13,000 feet of cumulative vertical ascent. There are also other similar desert events which are also extremely demanding such as the Gobi Desert in Outer Mongolia, over a distance of 140 miles in six days, with a five mile dune ridge walk to the finish on the seventh day. This involves mountain foothills, ice gorges and mountain gorges and desert plains, as well as the highest sand dunes in Asia.

What cannot be argued, however, is that the Marathon des Sables is an extremely demanding event, both physically and mentally. It is a multi-stage, self sufficiency event held in the Sahara desert. In other words it is held over a number of daily stages and during the event all competitors have to carry everything that they need for the duration of the event. (The only exceptions are a tent and water which are both provided.)

Traditionally the distance covered is between 140 and 150 miles, although it has in the past been as short as 128 miles in 1994. It is held in April in the Sahara, in the southern part of Morocco, and takes place over sand, stony and rocky trails and in dried ergs (from an Arabic word meaning "dune field" and referring to a large relatively flat area of desert covered with wind-swept sand with little or no vegetative cover) and wadis (the Arabic term traditionally refers to a valley but also refers to a dry riverbed that contains water only during times of heavy rain). It takes place over six days of competition, with a seventh day being included to either complete the long stage held on day four, or as a rest day if this stage has been completed in one day. The route changes from year to year and competitors are only informed of the exact route during the journey travelling out to the Sahara when road maps are issued. However, although it is often altered, the normal pattern is that the first three days cover distances of between 18 and 22 miles, before a long day of 45 to 50 miles. This is then followed by a standard marathon (26.2 miles) and a final day of between 10 and 13 miles.

In 2009 the event was held for the 24th time, having initially been staged in 1986 and having taken place without a break despite the difficulties imposed by The Gulf War in 1991, which saw the financial support disappear and the number of competitors reduced to 88, the third lowest number to have ever taken part.

The concept for the event was developed by Patrick Bauer, who has been the race director for all 24 runnings of the competition. In 1984, as a twenty-eight year old photographer, having had only three weeks of planning and preparation, he set off on 12th January with his brother and a friend, who accompanied him in a Peugeot 504, to cover a distance of approximately 218 miles, between Taanrasset and In Guezam. Unlike subsequent stagings of the event which evolved from this expedition there was no support team to provide water and he had to carry a backpack containing 15 litres of water, with a total weight of approximately 40 kilograms. Although the weight would be very unfamiliar to current entrants, the development of blisters is known to most. Those taking part in the event now also worry about whether they will have enough water, despite being provided with approximately 10 litres each day. With the addition of a further small supply of water, Patrick Bauer is said to have survived on 18 litres in total!

The event was born and the first formal Marathon des Sables commenced on 17th May 1986 with 23 participants, including two women. 10 to 15% of entrants subsequently have been female. The first ever winner was a Frenchman, Michel Galliez.

The Marathon des Sables may not have continued after the 3rd event in 1988 when the organisers and competitors had to deal with the emotional impact of the tragic death of one of the 162 competitors. The 28 year old collapsed after 12 miles on one of the stages when the temperature was a staggering 56º C. There has been one subsequent death in 2007 when a French competitor died after running the long stage. He had arrived back at his tent at 6.30pm and was in good condition. He had woken at 3.30am to welcome his tent mates back, and then tragically was found dead at 6.30am. Many people may consider that the death of two runners, albeit over a period of 24 years, is too high a price to pay for an amateur adventure. However, all those who take part are aware of the risk and choose to challenge themselves. The physical challenge is after all what the event is about. This death rate is actually impressively low bearing in mind that approximately 10,000 people have completed an event equivalent to approximately 5.5 marathons in extreme conditions. It is estimated that the death rate in a marathon is 1 in 50,000, a comparable figure. This death rate in itself is much lower than the equivalent death rate during the time period for completing a marathon for a group of non-competitors sitting at home and resting. The health benefits of training, physical exercise and competition far outweigh the small risk of injury, illness or tragically death.

It is perhaps in part as a response to such tragedies that the event has evolved to include a large number of rules and regulations with time penalties and potentially disqualification imposed for failing to comply.

They have also evolved in order to make absolutely certain that all competitors compete on an equal footing and that everyone carries all of their own equipment without any external support. All competitors, for example, must produce a medical certificate and a resting ECG carried out in the 28 days before the start. A list of compulsory equipment, mainly emphasising survival and safety, has been developed. Each competitor is responsible for providing their own food and has to be able to demonstrate that they are carrying a minimum of 2000 calories each day. Perhaps most importantly the organisers provide adequate water and emphasise the importance of rehydration. Failure to replace fluids will result in deterioration in performance, an inability to finish the event and in extreme cases renal failure, coma and death.

The full list of rules and time penalties is shown in figure 1. (The English translation from the French original does not always make it entirely clear what is meant!)

The event has also evolved in terms of the support team. It is only when actually taking part that it is possible to realise the scale of the organisation and the efficiency with which it operates. Over 800 competitors have to be supported for nine days and this requires an organisational team; course planners and markers; communication facilities; medical support; tents for all competitors and the support crew with a team of Berbers to put up, take down and reassemble the tents each day; the provision of fuel for the 4x4 vehicles and helicopters; as well as facilities for press and photographers. This whole team has to be adaptable, as was clearly demonstrated during this 24th running of the Marathon des Sables, when they responded to bizarre circumstances with commendable efficiency. Patrick Bauer, in 1984, was supported by his brother and a friend. By the time the event was staged in 2000, with 700 competitors, there were 180 organisation staff, as well as 80 4x4 vehicles, 2 helicopters, 1 Cessna aircraft and very importantly a 30 strong medical team.

These requirements have continued to increase and for this year (2009) involved:

- 100 volunteers on the course

1 – THE MARATHON DES SABLES

Reason for Penalty	Elimination	Time Penalty	Loss of deposit
More than 30 minutes delay at admin/tech check		Equal to lateness	
Missing document at technical checks	X		
Delay in sending administrative document		30 minutes	
Non submission of medical certificate and / or ECG	X If refused on medical grounds	1 hour + fixed fine	X If refused on medical grounds
No backpack or equivalent	X		X
No sleeping bag / compass with 1 or 2 degree precision		3 hours	
No survival kit (flare, stick lighter, road-book, salt tablets), 2000 calories per day, aluminium survival sheet		2 hours	
No 10 safety pins, knife with metal blade, whistle, antiseptic, mirror, aspi venom pump, steel flashlight+ batteries, pointing card, lighter		1 hour	
Incorrect weight of bag		1 hour	
Personal equipment element missing		30 minutes	
No number displayed	2nd time X	1st time – warning	2nd time X
Incorrectly positioned number	3rd time X	1st time-warning; 2nd time – 30 minutes	3rd time X
Tampering with ID	X		X
Lateness at start of stage		Equal to lateness	
Exceeding maximum allowed time	X		X
Out of time CP 3 "marathon" stage	X		X
Out of time CP4 "non-stop" stage	X		X
No check in at check point	3rd time X	1st time 1 hour 2nd time 2 hours	X
Failure to follow the markings		4 hours minimum	
Unjustified use of flares		1 hour	
Doping / use of transportation	X		X
Ground assistance	2nd time X	1st time 3 hours	2nd time X
Receiving of extra water	3rd time X	1st time 30 minutes; 2nd time 1 hour	3rd time X
Vital medical assistance	2nd time X	1st time 2 hours	2nd time X
Wandering far off course			X
Water and environment	3rd time X	1st time 30 minutes; 2nd time 1 hour	3rd time X

Figure 1 Summary of penalties

- 400 support staff overall
- 100,000 litres of mineral water
- 200 Berber and Saharan tents
- 100 all terrain vehicles
- 2 helicopters and 1 Cessna plane
- 19 buses
- 4 camels
- 1 incinerator lorry for burning rubbish
- 6 quad bikes
- 1 editing bus and 5 cameras
- 1 satellite image station
- 6 satellite telephones
- 15 computers, fax and internet

The support staff includes 42 members of the medical team, "Dr Trotters" as they are appropriately nicknamed, who remain an essential part of the organisation. Although much of their work, as their nickname implies, involves expert management of blisters, damaged toe nails and other foot problems, they also provide pain killers, anti-inflammatory drugs, dressings and in more extreme cases intravenous fluid replacement and other potentially lifesaving treatments.

In 2009 they provided:

- 4394 treatments
- 18 intravenous infusions
- 3450 analgesic tablets
- 3200 anti-inflammatory drugs
- 1.8 kilometres of plasters
- 82 litres of antiseptic
- 2000 pairs of gloves

The organisation now also includes everything that is expected in modern day communication. Although this may reduce the sense of isolation and adventure and limit the ability to completely escape from the normal pressures created by living in the 21st century, it is a welcome facility for most. There is an email tent and each entrant can send one email a day to one address. A telephone tent allows phone calls to friends and family, and many take their own mobile phones with them, although fortunately, for those of us who want to get away from civilisation, reception is not always that good. Perhaps the most important and welcome communication is the facility arranged by the organisers to receive emails from home. These are printed out and delivered to each tent at the end of each day and are looked forward to with great anticipation, and often read with the shedding of a few tears. During the 23rd Marathon des Sables 39,885 emails were received and distributed.

The organisers take their responsibility to the environment very seriously and as much waste as possible is destroyed at the base camp after the bivouac has been taken down, using a unique auto-combustion incinerator lorry. Each competitor has to also take responsibility for their own potentially damaging impact on the environment and time penalties are imposed if bottles of water are not disposed of correctly. To facilitate this since the 8th Marathon des Sables, each bottle, and each bottle top, is marked with the competitor's race number before being handed out.

Toilets are installed for competitors, using biodegradable products that help dissolve human waste. For those who smoke, presumably a small number, small pocket ashtrays are provided to get rid of cigarette stubs. (I found these a very convenient way of carrying each day's supply of salt tablets.)

The organisers also contribute to the support and development of the local communities. In 1993 a competitor, Gilles Flamant, worked with the Marathon des Sables organisation to develop a water pump in the village of Ighef n'rifi. Powered by the sun the pump was able to produce 25 cubic metres of pure water each day for the children and adults of the village. The success in this village has led to the development of pumps in other villages.

In the village of Jdaid, a craft cooperative, a crèche and a clinic were built in 2007. Since then a kitchen, meeting room, office and treatment room have been added. The project improves the position of women within the village and encourages people to continue to live in the desert.

The last phase of the project will include an irrigation network, water and sanitation works and the extension of the medical area.

The organisation team are responsible for not only planning the course but for marking it out. Yellow signs are placed along the course the night before each stage and checked again the following morning. Compass points are provided on these boards and also in the road book issued to each competitor. At night time a green fluorescent light is placed on each of the signs and a laser shines out from the penultimate check point to guide those taking part. In addition on the night stage all competitors carry an orange fluorescent stick in the back of their rucksack to act as a guide for the following competitors. There are numerous marshals, many of whom are volunteers, who as well as manning check-points situated at intervals of approximately 10 kilometres, also travel around the course in 4x4 vehicles. With all this guidance it is difficult to understand how it is possible to wander more than a short distance away from the planned route.

However, in 1994, one of the 127 competitors went missing. The long stage was 43 miles and due to a sandstorm the stage was interrupted at the fifth check-point after 35 miles. It was then discovered that an Italian had not been seen since the third check-point at 24 miles, which, as a good runner, he had reached among the first 20 competitors. Despite an extensive search involving helicopters and numerous vehicles over several days the only trace was a pair of socks, a rocket launcher without the distress rockets, food wrappers and his road book, until he was eventually located nine days later in hospital in Tindouf in Algeria. He personally claimed that he survived without water and by eating snakes and drinking his own urine. A fictional account was eventually produced and shot in the desert with him as the star. The organisers believe that he did indeed get lost after check-point 3, but the rest of his claims and the length of time of his disappearance seem unlikely in some minds.

There are probably as many reasons for entering the event as there are entrants. The elite athletes are interested in competing and racing not only for the prestige of winning the event but also attracted by the prize money.

- 1st prize   trophy and 5000 Euros   (4000 Euros for women)
- 2nd prize   trophy and 3000 Euros   (2000 Euros for women)
- 3rd prize   trophy and 1500 Euros   (1000 Euros for women)
- 4th prize to 10th   trophy and 500 Euros towards next entry

In addition there are prizes for teams and in the veteran categories.

Others, although experienced runners and walkers, will never be among the winners, but having completed marathons and ultra-marathons now want to challenge themselves and push themselves to explore their personal limits. Others, sometimes with no or minimal experience, are attracted by the event itself, having read about it, seen it on television or informed by friends who have taken part. Others enter in a spirit of bravado, often after a few drinks, and then have to face the reality of what may well be the greatest challenge of their lives.

No matter what the original reason, all competitors will have to face up to the challenge of preparing themselves for this event, and then more importantly face the experience of stepping outside of their comfort zone and competing in an environment which very few will have ever faced before. The challenge of taking part in an extremely tough event in a potentially inhospitable environment while being responsible for everything required to survive for a week is a major contrast to the lifestyle and circumstances which most people face in the 21st century. The experience of living for a week in the desert with a group of likeminded individuals and enjoying the camaraderie which develops, acts as a lure for some who return to the event over and over again. (Perhaps one of the most bizarre examples of camaraderie and support for other competitors occurred during the 14th event when a female competitor gave her knickers, hopefully a fresh pair, to a male entrant to protect his head from sun burn.)

There is obviously a risk element and this is accepted by all who take part. The risk is minimised by adequate training and preparation, by the rules and regulations and by the efforts of the organisers. However, the risk cannot be totally eliminated and in a society which appears to have become risk averse, this component of the event is probably an underlying reason why many take part and is part of the overall challenge. Since the race commenced in 1986 over 10,000 people have taken part and the vast majority have finished the event. The dropout rate is extremely low. In 2008 53 out of a starting number of 800 had to drop out and for 2009 42 out of a starting field of 812 dropped out. The 10,000 plus competitors have included:

- 30% repeat competitors
- 14% women
- 45% veterans
- 10% walkers
- 8.7 miles per hour the average maximum speed
- 1.85 miles per hour the average minimum speed
- Youngest competitor age 16
- Oldest competitor age 78

The event has been dominated at the sharp end since 1992 by the Ahansal brothers. Lahcen, a carpenter from Zagora, with little experience and poor equipment finished in third place in 1992, missing out on second position because of a time penalty imposed as he did not have the compulsory anti-venom pump. He followed this in 1994 with a fifth position, and then in 1996 with very little training he was not able to complete the event. The following year he and his brother Mohamad, a mountain guide, finished fourth and fifth, until eventually in 1997 Lahcen won the eleventh event. They have since dominated the event with Lahcen winning on 10 occasions and Mohamad on three occasions, including his victory this year in the 24th Marathon des Sables. Lahcen had to withdraw during the long stage at checkpoint 4.

At the other extreme are those who walk the whole event, but who nevertheless are winners, in that they have accepted and completed their personal challenge. In some ways this event is harder for these competitors who spend much longer on their feet with a correspondingly shorter recovery time but, while being out on the trail for much longer, still receive the same water supplies as faster runners. There are numerous heroic tales of those who have taken part. Perhaps one of the most striking is that of Claude Compain, who first took part in the tenth event in 1996 at the age of seventy-two and subsequently ran in 1997, 1998 and 1999. After his first event the organisers gave him the number corresponding to his age.

Another interesting note in regard to race numbers is that one year a female competitor wore the number 13 and broke her leg during the event. Since then the number has not been used unless it is specifically requested.

CHAPTER TWO

MOROCCO AND THE SAHARA DESERT

The Marathon des Sables is held in Morocco, officially the Kingdom of Morocco. Morocco is situated in the North Eastern corner of Africa, but has strong historical links with Spain and has expressed a wish to join the European Union. Its western border is the coastline on the Atlantic Ocean which extends past the Strait of Gibraltar into the Mediterranean Sea. It has borders with Algeria to the east, Mauritania to the south and Spain to the north.

Morocco has a population of nearly 34 million, almost 40 per cent of whom are under 15 years old. This population inhabits the 275,000 square miles that constitutes Morocco, although it is unevenly distributed with the majority living along the Atlantic coast and in the Rif and High Atlas mountains.

Morocco is covered by sand dunes, rocky terrain, dry lakes and wadis, jebels and the snow covered Atlas Mountains.

Moroccan Arabic, an Arabic vernacular, is the most common native language. Amazigh or Berber languages are also widely spoken. French is widely used in the government in official texts, and in the business community, though in neither instance is this 'official'. Morocco is a constitutional monarchy with its king Mohammed VI and its Prime Minister Abbas El Fassi. 80 per cent of the population is Arab and 20% Berber.

OUARZAZATE

Ouarzazate (pronounced War-za-zat), in the south east between the snow capped Atlas Mountains and the Sahara, is situated in the valley of the River Ouarzazate near its juncture with the River Drâa. It is the traditional starting point for the Marathon des Sables and competitors arrive at its airport before spending the night in a local hotel. Ouarzazate is the most important of the southern towns and is strategically located at a crossroads that joins the north to the south and the east to the west. Ouarzazate is a good location from which to explore as far afield as Zagora, Agdz, Skoura, Tineghir and the Todra Gorge and dozens of breathtaking kasbahs.

Ouarzazate has a population of about 40,000 inhabitants. Its focal point is the long and wide street Avenue Muhammad V. Ouarzazate is designed for tourism, and is well established with numerous hotels of high standard, but relatively few restaurants. There is a strange and empty feeling to Ouarzazate, except in the centre where a typical Moroccan market dominates. The Kasbah of Ouarzazate is said to "stand out as an example of how to take care of heritage with style" and has been used in numerous films.

Ouarzazate is home of one of the largest film studios in the world, Atlas Studios, and is sometimes referred to as the Moroccan Hollywood. Several historical movies have been produced here, including Asterix & Obelix, Mission Cleopatra, Lawrence of Arabia, The Man Who Would Be King, Cleopatra, Kundun, Gladiator and lately Alexander, Kingdom of Heaven and Babel. The studio is situated outside of the town and is open to the public for tours.

ERFOUD

Erfoud does not normally feature in the Marathon des Sables but for the 24th event it became an important base for two days due to the bizarre and unexpected weather which delayed the start of the event.

Erfoud, sometimes referred to as "the door of the Sahara", was founded as a military outpost to bring the Bedouins in the region under French control in Morocco. Erfoud is now used as a base for tourists wishing to explore the Ziz valley, and the dunes at Merzouga. It has a population of less than 10,000.

Located on the Ziz River, it was built in the early 1900s by the French as an administrative headquarters. Its buildings are made from the red sand of the area mixed with lime. The settlement with its high walls and tightly packed houses was constructed as protection from the marauding nomadic tribes.

Erfoud has a flourishing marble industry. Marble from the area is red, brown and black. Erfoud is also renowned for its fossils.

In the area around Erfoud almost a million date palms grow and each year during the October harvest, the date festival, lasting for three days, is held. The festival is an occasion for the region's tribes and innkeepers to get together in a typical setting. Accompanied by music, among the Berber tents, the traditional gesture of welcome, a glass of tea is offered.

Dates, with their sweet taste, are regarded as a symbol of 'Good Luck' and so are a common feature in gifts and ceremonies, being offered to friends and strangers alike. The festival includes music, traditional processions and dance and following a fashion parade the award of the title of 'Miss Date'.

THE SAHARA DESERT

The Marathon des Sables is run in the Sahara desert, which many consider to be the largest and hottest desert in the world. Although it is the hottest, it is not the largest, with this honour going to Antarctica. Despite being only the second largest desert it still covers around 9,000,000 square kilometres, an area as large as the United States of America, and accounts for 8 per cent of the world's land area. It covers almost eleven countries, including Algeria, Chad, Egypt, Libya, Morocco,

Mauritania, Mali, Niger, Sudan, Tunisia and Western Sahara.

The Sahara stretches from the Atlantic Ocean on the West, the Atlas Mountains and the Mediterranean Sea in the North, The Red Sea and Egypt on the East, and the Sudan and the valley of the Niger River in the South. The boundaries, however, are not clearly defined, and have been shifting for a thousand years. The Sahara was once a fertile area; millet and other grains were cultivated there over 8000 years ago.

The landscape obviously includes massive sand dunes which can reach a height of almost 190 metres, but there are also large stony plateaus, gravel plains, dry valleys and sand flats.

The temperature during the hottest periods of the year can exceed 50°C, although in the winter months the temperature can drop below freezing, and the peaks during the winter can be snow-capped. It receives only eight inches of rainfall each year. Despite these huge temperature variations the Sahara is home to a number of different animals. Camels and goats are the well known domesticated animals living here, but the Saharan cheetah, sand vipers, scorpions and lizards are also endemic. As well as this diversity of animal life there are also around 500 species of flora, consisting mainly of short-lived plants known locally as Acheb. Olive trees abound in some areas.

Despite the hostile environment, the Sahara is home to nomadic groups who are mainly engaged in trading and hunting. Farming is carried out in parts of the Sahara producing drought-resistant plants and some areas have been transformed to prevent soil erosion. The total population of the Sahara is no more than 2 million.

It is in this harsh environment that the Marathon des Sables has been held every year for 24 years.

PART TWO

MY TRAINING

CHAPTER THREE

INITIAL TRAINING AND MOVING TO ULTRA MARATHONS

There are numerous guides and programmes for anyone planning to run a 10k, a half marathon or a full marathon. These training programmes are often underpinned by a lot of scientific evidence and anecdotal experience. There is, however, very little information as to how to train for an event such as the Marathon des Sables. There is also much less scientific evidence and what is available is often of poor quality or even contradictory.

How then does a potential competitor approach their training? This will obviously depend upon a number of factors. Some of those taking part will have had many years of training and competing, whereas others will have decided they want to face the challenge of the Marathon des Sables and commence their training purely for this event. Some competitors will only be interested in getting round, hopefully in one piece, and completing the challenge. Others will be interested in actively competing and will be concerned about their position and time. Finally some people will have as much time as is needed to train, while others will have to balance the demands of training against other facets of their life such as work, family and other competing interests.

This account is very much my personal account and is not intended as a recipe for potential entrants to the Marathon des Sables or similar multi-stage ultra events. It certainly worked for me but may well be totally inappropriate for others.

My background is of many years experience of running, having done my first marathon in 1986. Between 1989, when I fractured my pelvis in four places following a horse riding accident, and 2005 when I recommenced serious training in preparation for the Inaugural Antarctic Ice Marathon, I had continued to run on a regular basis but at a much lower weekly mileage. My running had to be balanced against my family commitments, my professional life as a general medical practitioner and my other interests of horse riding and golf.

By the time I commenced to train for the Marathon des Sables I had retired as a principal in General Practice and was working part time as a salaried GP with much more time available to train. My family had left home and my wife, Cherith, is fortunately very understanding and supportive. During the final six months before the Marathon des Sables I devoted all of my effort to training and preparation and virtually stopped playing golf and riding my horse.

There were a number of principles that underlined my training for this event in comparison to how I would normally prepare for a marathon or a shorter distance.

Firstly, I was aware that while running in the Marathon des Sables it would be necessary to be used to being on my feet for a long time. This was not going to be achieved by a series of low mileage runs, no matter how beneficial high intensity training sessions of this type might be. I decided it would be necessary to gradually increase the time in training that I spent on my feet so that I could readily cope with training sessions lasting for ten hours.

Secondly, I realised that for me much of the event would be carried out at a walking pace and not running. The act of walking places different strains on the legs and different frictional forces on the feet. If I was going to be able to cope with the demands of the Marathon des Sables while limiting the risk of injuries and the likelihood of blisters I needed to change much of my training, which traditionally was all running, and incorporate a lot of walking. This second strategy tied in with the first one of long training sessions. It would not be possible to be on my feet and running for up to ten hours without overtraining and risking injury or illness.

Thirdly, this event was a multi-stage event in which one long day is followed by another equally long, or even longer, day. Traditionally after running a marathon it is considered necessary to have a period of rest and recuperation for two to three weeks. I had to get used to a different approach and do back-to-back sessions of long mileage days in order to mimic in training the requirements of the race.

Fourthly, although I was taking part in an event in which the shortest day would be approximately a half-marathon distance and although I would not be interested in running fast, there is good evidence that even for marathons and ultra marathons there are benefits from training at a faster pace than the projected event pace. It was therefore necessary to incorporate tempo sessions (run at just greater than my 10K pace), and interval sessions where a series of runs varying between 400 metres and 1 mile are alternated with recovery jogs.

Fifthly, I needed to incorporate gym sessions and core muscle sessions into my regular programme. I do not particularly enjoy either of these two types of sessions, and particularly the core muscle sessions. However, high repetition, low weight muscle training would reduce the risk of lower limb injuries and would also strengthen my upper body in readiness for carrying a 10kg (22lbs), or heavier, rucksack. The core muscle sessions, strengthening abdominal, lower back and buttock muscles, would be important to reduce the risk of back problems and also to reduce the risk of injury caused by muscle fatigue and loss of form while running long distances.

It is difficult to state exactly when I started to train for the Marathon des Sables. Over a period of time my normal regular training gradually increased with increasing mileage in each session and a gradual increase in my total weekly mileage, and I gradually began to adapt my training for this specific event following the strategy outlined above.

As can be seen in figure 2 at the beginning of 2008 I was running approximately 40 miles per week. I had decided it would be sensible to

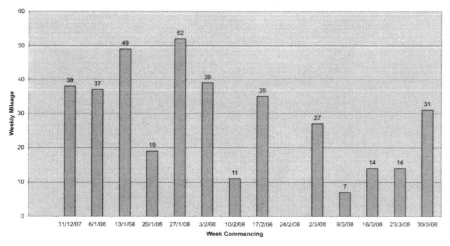

Figure 2 Weekly mileage January 2008 to March 2008

tackle my first ultra marathon. (An ultra marathon is any distance over the standard marathon distance of 26.2 miles.) In preparation, I ran the Gloucester marathon on 27th January 2008. My aim was to combine walking and running, alternating 8 minutes running with 2 minutes walking. It was unseasonably hot and I was able to run in a T-shirt. I was slowing down towards the end but was happy to finish in a time of 4 hours and 20 minutes.

I deliberately did not leave myself a two to three week recovery period but continued to train in readiness for the ultra marathon I had chosen which fell three weeks later and was held at Draycote Water Country Park, near Kenilworth. The race was over 35 miles on a flat course involving multiple laps round the roughly five mile private perimeter road. The course was virtually traffic free with the added attraction of wildlife on the water. The other advantage was the ability to return approximately every five miles to the starting area to my support team (consisting of my wife, Cherith, and later in the race our friends Andy and Rosemary Skilbeck) to take on water, bananas, jelly babies and carbohydrate gels and bars. I was not certain how I would cope after the 26 mile mark and so I deliberately set myself a target of a steady pace with the aim of finishing inside the cut off time of 6 hours and 30 minutes. I was pleased to complete my first ultra in a time of 6 hours 29 minutes and 12 seconds, which suggests I got my pacing absolutely right.

The period from April to June 2008 involved me continuing to run an average of about 35 miles each week. Figure 3 shows a number of gaps in data as I did not always run with my Garmin watch, and I also had a two week period with a hamstring injury. Apart from that I remained remarkably injury free over the 15 months leading up to the Marathon des Sables. On 11th May I took part in the annual Beaverbrook 10K on Blackpool promenade, which I have now run on numerous occasions. I was delighted with my time of 45 minutes as this meant an improvement of nearly five minutes on the time that I had done in 2007. It also gave me a predicted time for the marathon of sub 3 hours 30 minutes (I would be delighted if I could manage such a time!).

A key point in my training was on 25th July 2008 when I attended "Sportstest" in the West Midlands for formal testing by a sports physiologist. This test showed an impressively low body fat of 7.7% (the figure for the normal male population is between 12 and 15%) and a sub-maximal VO2 of 43.24 l/min. The main point to come out of the testing

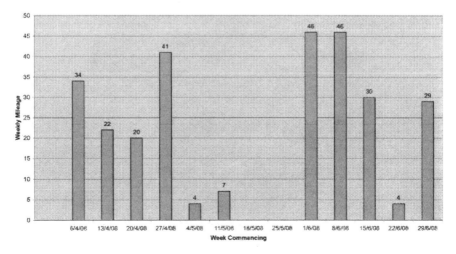

Figure 3   Weekly mileage April 2008 to June 2008

was a need to concentrate on base training. In other words I needed to run a lot of miles at a slow pace, making sure I kept my pulse rate at my measured endurance level of between 130 and 140 beats per minute. From that point I ran regularly with a heart rate monitor. It was at this stage that I also incorporated the approach of "periodisation". Basically this involved me gradually increasing my mileage over three consecutive weeks and then having a fourth low mileage week. This fourth week was to allow for recovery and reduce the risk of injury. The next four week period would involve an increase in weekly mileage in comparison with the immediate preceding period. This pattern shows in Figure 4, although with some variation due to the need to adapt my weekly training to take into account other demands on my time.

On the 9th August I wrote in my blog "This weeks training ended today with a 14 mile endurance paced run. Got up and ready to set off this morning when the skies opened with torrential rain. Decided to wait for it to ease off – but it didn't – may have some sand storms in the Sahara but no rain like this fortunately. [Little did I know when I wrote this entry in my blog what I was actually going to face at the start of the Marathon

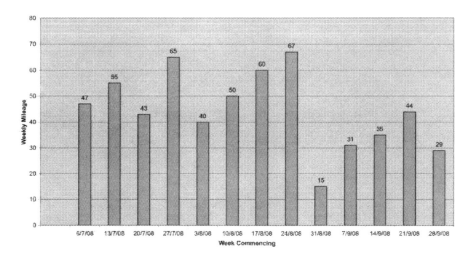

Figure 4 Weekly mileage July 2008 to September 2008

des Sables!] Eventually decided to run on my treadmill. I find this so boring and was tempted to stop more than once but managed to do the planned 14 miles – the furthest I have ever run on a treadmill in one go."

The last week in August was planned as a high mileage week. I started off with the Fleetwood half marathon on 24th August, which I deliberately ran slowly – about 2 minutes per mile slower than my normal pace, for 2 reasons. Firstly I was training using a heart rate monitor keeping my heart rate between 130 and 140 in order to develop a good base level of endurance fitness. Secondly I was using the "race" as the first part of a long run and ran home after the event, making a total distance of just over 24 miles. I recovered well and managed to carry on with the rest of my training programme that week. Saturday, however, was a real effort. I was not sure if that was the effect of the high mileage week – 70 miles in total, the rather muggy weather, the fact that I was running with a back pack for only the second time or the curry and red wine on Friday night – probably a combination of all of these!

The difficulty I faced in this last training session of the week demonstrated to me that training for this event was not just about getting myself prepared physically but also, and possibly more importantly, about mental training. It would have been very easy to cut that run short and call it a day. However, that would not be possible half way through the 50 mile day in the Sahara, unless I was not going to finish the long day in one go, or not complete the whole event which was not part of my plan. I wrote in my blog, "I am sure there will be times [during the event] when I will wonder why I am doing it and will want to stop, so mentally difficult days like yesterday when I have to push myself to continue are all part of the mental toughness that will be needed."

The weather in early September was horrendous and resulted in an alteration to my running plans. I was planning to run the 40 mile Coventry Way on 7th September. The weather was so bad with flood warnings in the Midlands that I decided to stay at home. My intention had been to then run in the Great Langdale Marathon the following Sunday but to just do the half marathon distance. So as I had not done the 40 mile run I decided to have a go at the full marathon distance. I nearly didn't even make the start due to the heavy traffic in Windermere! The Langdale Marathon is described as the "world's toughest road marathon" and after about one mile I realised why. A one in three incline for about a mile made me decide very early on to walk the uphill sections and run the level stretches and downhill. My intention was to take it nice and steady and see how I felt after the first half and to decide if to continue (the marathon is 2 laps). Despite the hills I felt really good at the half way point, and felt it had not taken anything out of me. I did the second half at a quicker pace (2hrs 20 compared with 2 hours 27), overtook 18 people and was not overtaken by anyone. I felt really good at the end and felt I could have run further.

I had not intended to take part but was aware of the High Peak 40, which took place the following Sunday (21st September). As its name implies the run / walk is over 40 miles in the Peak District taking in Mam Tor. As I felt so good after the Great Langdale marathon and had recovered very quickly I decided to give it a go. The race set off from Buxton at 8am. I bumped into Wendy McKinnon who was also running and who I last saw in Antarctica. What a beautiful run – and a good job, because it was incredibly tough. Without doubt at that time the toughest run I have ever done. My GPS watch showed approximately 7500 feet of ascent – that's like climbing Snowdon twice, as well as running over 40 miles!

I managed to get lost after about 23 miles due to a missing road sign; at least I didn't see it! This added about 1.5 miles to the total distance and almost made me give up. I was about to phone Cherith, who was supporting me, when I bumped into another runner's wife, who kindly gave me a lift back to where I had gone wrong. I managed to get to Tideswell which was the marathon distance and told Cherith I was going to carry on a bit further, but didn't think that I would finish. However, I got my second wind and by the next checkpoint at 29 miles I was determined to finish. Another lesson learned – keep going through the bad patches and you will get your second wind – hopefully!

As I say, at the time, probably the toughest thing I have done! Some of the hills were incredibly steep and long and it was impossible (for me) to run the whole way. At about 36 miles there was a horrible ravine, which it was difficult to pick my way down – and then back up the other side. This was followed by a series of stiles. I felt at times I could only just about pick my legs up high enough to get over them and got to the stage that I never wanted to see a stile again. I wasn't helped by a large blister on my heel – this had initially started at Great Langdale and became much larger and more painful on this run.

I managed to get to the end – and actually was running quite strongly at the finish – in a total time of 10 hours and 50 minutes. A great experience as time on my feet is so important and a big psychological boost to manage a very tough marathon and then 6 days later a hilly 40 miler (which turned out for me with my various detours to be nearer 44 miles), the furthest distance I have ever done. I was encouraged by the way my training was going and I still had 6 months to go.

I was able to head out to our apartment in Tenerife in late September for some slightly warmer weather training. In the first week I deliberately ran a "half Marathon des Sables" – not just in terms of the distance but mimicking the pattern of the real event with each day being half of the equivalent day in the Marathon des Sables with a rest day after the long run.

As a result I ran 75 miles in total, divided up as 8 miles, 10 miles, 12 miles, 25 miles, rest day, 13 miles and 7 miles. The big one was on Wednesday when I did 25 miles. I planned to get up early and head up to Teide National Park which is about an hour away from our apartment. Mount Teide is the highest mountain in Spain at 3718 metres. I left at 7am for "warm weather training" – but the closer I got and the higher I went the lower the temperature became. According to the gauge in my car it started dropping into single figures and before I parked up the ice warning light had come on in the car and the temperature was 2°C! It had risen to 7°C by the time I set off – wearing 2 shirts and a hat, which I had intended to use to protect me from the sun!

Despite the temperature I had a great run in beautiful scenery, although still in shade for the first seven miles and I was desperate for the sun to shine where I was actually running. I did not see anyone for ten miles from Parador, running along tracks by the side of volcanic mountains, until I reached my turn around point at El Portillo where I got a further supply of water at the visitor's centre. It was another seven miles back along the same track before I saw anyone else. I got back to the car after 20 miles, where I did a quick inspection of my feet and, as there were no signs of any blisters, I did another section of just under five miles to make the total distance of 25 miles. The temperature in the car on my return was 30°C; a variation of 23 degrees from starting to finishing!

What was particularly pleasing was that I was running not only on rough terrain and in the heat but at an altitude of about 7000 feet for my long run. Also, during this week of my mini Marathon des Sables, all of my runs were with a pack on my back – even if only weighing about 3kgs (6.6lbs) at this stage.

So half a Marathon des Sables in heat and with a pack – and 6 months to go, so I felt I was well on schedule with my planned training. I had hoped to do another half Marathon des Sables the following week but ended up doing a slightly shorter distance, but still managed just over 55 miles, which was pleasing on the back of the previous high mileage week.

My return home and continued training was with a total contrast in the weather. Despite the change in weather I was able to keep up a high mileage, with a 20 mile run on the Sunday and finished the week with 25.5 miles on Saturday, and both runs carrying my back pack which I will be using in the Marathon des Sables, weighing about 4 to 4.5kgs (9 or 10lbs). It was important to start to get used to carrying a rucksack and gradually increase the weight. The other days in the week between these two longer runs consisted of a rest day on Monday, 6miles on Tuesday and 11.5 on each of Wednesday and Thursday, before a further rest day on Friday. My total distance was 74 miles – and I was looking forward to a rest week, relatively speaking!

For those who know the Fylde Coast my run on the Sunday had set off from home, out to the path around the De Vere hotel and across Marton Mere and out to the motorway. I then ran to Ballam and ended up on the sea front at Lytham and then running along the promenade at

St Annes where I bought some more water to top up my supplies before continuing along the beach to Squires Gate. I then made my way back via Highfied Road, Cherry Tree Road and Preston Old Road, finishing with the track around the De Vere hotel and then back to home.

The 25.5 mile session on the Saturday was on 25th October when I took part in the Long Distance Walking Association 23 miles "Bottoms Up", taking in Hoghton Bottoms, Salmesbury Bottoms and the surrounding fells. The weather was awful – strong winds, heavy rain for a lot of the run and as most of it was off road a lot of mud, and then some more. And so many stiles that I got to the stage when I did not want to see a field or a stile for a long time. I initially tried to pick my way through the worst areas of mud and free lying water but I eventually realised it was a waste of time and so just ran through whatever was in front of me with cold water and mud coming up over my shoes and ankles. I had instructions for the route but still managed to get lost on a few occasions so the 23 miles ended up for me as 25.5 miles. I nearly ended up without any instructions as I had forgotten to take anything to protect my map from the rain and by 14 miles it was rapidly deteriorating to an almost illegible pulp! I will be forever grateful to the walker who gave me his protected copy or I might never have got off the fells. This event was held on the same day as the OMM (Original Mountain Marathon) in the Lake District which hit national television and newspapers because of the horrendous conditions. It also faced totally inappropriate criticism from the media who were after a story which never existed.

CHAPTER FOUR

TRAINING PHASE 2 – UPPING THE TEMPO

At the beginning of November I moved into Phase 2 of my training and as can be seen from Figure 5 my weekly mileage increased.

The plan was to gradually increase my mileage but include some "quality" sessions in which I would increase my pulse rate to my threshold level, between 150 and 160. The intention, which I achieved, was to gradually increase my mileage to a maximum of 100 miles per week with most of my runs still at a slow steady pace. I realised it would be difficult to get so many miles in each week, and I needed to do two training sessions on Monday and Wednesday for a number of weeks. It was tough to get up and set off for the first training session while it was still dark but I had got to the stage where I was no longer running because I enjoyed it but because I needed to train. I could have avoided two training sessions per day if I had run every day of the week but I wanted to continue to have two rest days. The rest days are as important a part of training as the running, allowing my body to recover and rebuild to move on and gradually increase my training levels. I had just hit 58 as I moved into this phase of my training, so rest days were particularly important to reduce the risk of injury or illness, either of which scenarios could have been a real problem as the race was getting closer and the time for recovery was limited

4 – TRAINING PHASE 2

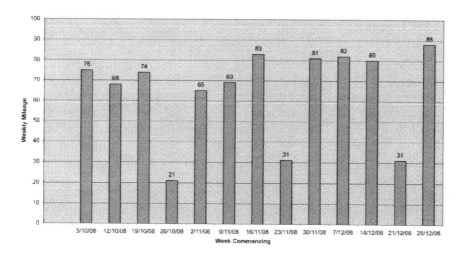

Figure 5   Weekly mileage October 2008 to December 2008

In terms of the quality sessions I planned to add one per week initially but move onto two per week. These would be either:

- a tempo session of 4 to 5 miles at a pace 20 seconds per mile greater than my 10 K race pace – so for me that was about 7minutes 35 seconds per mile (with 1-2 miles warm up and cool down at the beginning and end of each session)
- a hill session – fast pace up hill (heart rate 150-160) and recover when running down hill – repeated over planned distance

    OR

- an interval session – variable planned distances at the same heart rate as for hill sessions with recovery jogs over a distance which was based on how far the faster intervals were and again with warm up and cool down.

I was also planning, as one of the slow steady sessions, if possible once per week, to do a really long session with a pack on my back. This session would be mainly walking and the aim was to get me used to being on my feet for a long time and carrying a pack on my back. It was not going to be possible to run all of the Marathon des Sables so walking training was going to be important. I started this approach at the beginning of November with seven to eight hours and about 5.5kgs (12lbs) weight and increased gradually over the next four months.

The first week of phase two went well, despite some awful weather. I managed to get in 72 miles, starting with 18 miles on Sunday, followed by 8 miles before work on Monday (one of the advantages of being semi-retired!), as the first of my two sessions that day. Wednesday saw another early morning session and then a "quality" run later in the afternoon. This session was eight miles in total with the four miles either side of a two mile warm up and a two mile cool down at an increased tempo pace. I did wonder as I set off if it may have been a bit too far and fast for my first tempo run for a few months but it went very well and I felt very comfortable. I managed a further eight miles on Thursday.

Friday 7th November saw my first long day walking with a back pack. I set off with almost 6kgs (13lbs) on my back at just after 8am. I initially walked with my two training companions – Della and BB; but as they are boxer dogs they won't be doing the Marathon des Sables with me. I did just over two miles with the dogs before returning home and then I set off again immediately retracing my steps through Todderstaffe Farm and across the fields to Poulton. Then via Breck Road I headed to River Wyre and walked along the edge of the river through Stannah and behind ICI at Thornton. I headed west to the sea front at Cleveleys and then walked – partly on the beach and partly on the promenade to Squires Gate. I headed back inland through Marton and around the golf course at the De Vere hotel, and then via Staining to home. In order to make up the total mileage I then set off again with the dogs for a final 2 miles.

The aim was to be on my feet for about eight hours. It turned out to be 7 hours and 40 minutes – but I did not have the energy or the enthusiasm to carry on for another 20 minutes. I had expected to do about 27 or 28 miles in eight hours and was pleased that I actually did 30 miles

4 – TRAINING PHASE 2

in the time I was out. Over the last two hours or so, my legs and back were screaming at me to stop. I realised I should have been walking at a slower pace and so reduced my speed, as the main purpose of the exercise was to be on my feet for a long spell, not to cover as far as possible in the eight hour time period.

After a soak in the bath (I cannot remember the last bath I had as I prefer showers), I actually had a lie down on my bed for an hour or so as I had to recharge my batteries for a bonfire party that night. I am not sure that standing for three hours was the best way to end the day, but a very pleasant evening anyway.

On 23rd November I updated my blog with the following entry:

"I have been getting in some good training and managed 79 miles and 84 miles over the last two weeks. I don't think I have ever done more than 80 miles in a week before! I was a bit concerned after my initial long day walking when I did 30 miles as my legs felt so sore. However, the last two weeks I have increased this to 32 and 34 miles at the same time as increasing the weight in my bag to 7kgs (15.5lbs) and then 7.5kgs (16.5lbs). Both walks have gone really well and I have felt fine at the end and recovered well.

"Last week was a bit odd as I had to do two days with double training sessions. The first was on Sunday when my plan had initially been for a 22 mile run. However I also had tickets to watch Blackpool FC playing Preston North End, which kicked off at 1 o'clock. I decided that rather than getting up and setting off when it was still dark, that I would do 18 miles in the morning, go to the match and then do six miles in the late afternoon. It's a pity that the Blackpool players were not able to show the same level of commitment! Also I was not able to fit in a run on Wednesday, so I did a double session on Thursday. Saturday would normally be a rest day but I decided to do a short run with my bag on my back, although at a reduced weight of 5kgs (11lbs). It seemed really odd when I set off, as this was the first run as opposed to walk with more than a few pounds on my back, and I wondered how on earth I would manage 150 miles at 40º C carrying over 10kgs (22lbs). However after about one mile I settled into a rhythm and it actually felt quite comfortable in the end.

"My 32 mile long walk wreaked a bit of havoc with my feet. I have decided that I will almost certainly be running in UK Gear's desert shoes, having found them so good when training in Tenerife, so I decided to give their Winter shoes a try. They seemed OK but obviously just a little too small and over 32 miles they resulted in bruised nails and blisters. One blister is right next to the nail and has worked under the nail adjacent to the nail bed. Fairly painful and am going to lose the first nail ever after many years of running. Good experience for learning how to look after my feet and manage blisters next year.

"I contacted UK Gear and am delighted by their excellent service. The shoes have been replaced at no extra charge for a half size bigger and I used them for my 34 mile walk with no deterioration, so hopefully they will be OK. It is nice to deal with a company which values customer service."

The next week was a recovery low mileage week which I finished off in Tenerife with a few four to six mile runs, which were really enjoyable, as the weather was warmer and it was a pleasure to run in shorts and shirt, rather than leggings and a waterproof and windproof long sleeved top. The first day of the next period of training happened to be the best day of the whole week that we had in Tenerife with temperatures which must have been at least in the mid 20s, if not higher. I planned to do a 20 mile run and to carry about 6kgs (just over 13lbs) in my rucksack. The intention was to take some water with me and then buy some more in Las Galletas, a small town about five miles from our apartment, and so I put a 10 euro note in my bag. The first problem was before I left the apartment when I realised that the bottles of "still water" were actually sparkling water – not the best for when out running. I added Nunn tablets (electrolyte replacement) to the bottles and set off. I had not even got down the first flight of stairs when there was an explosion and the top flew off one of the bottles under the pressure from the combined effects of the sparkling water and the effervescent Nunn tablets. It would be the bottle that was lying horizontally across the front pack of my rucksack at waist level, and so all the contents spilled down my shorts and legs and onto the stair well. A quick replacement with tap water and I set off again.

I did not drink enough as I started the run – I do not think I realised quite how hot it was as the first few days had not been brilliant. I got to Las Galletas and discovered that I had not put the 10 euro note in my bag! I started to eke out my water supply, hoping it would last for my planned 20 mile training session. The first bottle lasted me for 10 miles – the following day which was much cooler it lasted for just under five miles! By this time I had run from Palm Mar across the nature reserve, through Las Galletas and out to Golf del Sur. I turned round to head back home and had to discipline myself not to gulp all my water supply but to ration it out. After 15 miles my energy levels were seriously depleted, as can be expected with dehydration, and I had to start walking. At 16 miles I phoned Cherith to ask her to come out to meet me with some water as I was literally down to my last mouthful! By this time I was near the lighthouse, just two miles from our apartment, and so I decided to head back directly to Palm Mar, rather than the longer route that I had planned which was a further four miles. Fortunately I bumped into Martyn and Angela whom we have got to know since going out to Tenerife regularly and they kindly let me have some of their water, and shortly after Cherith arrived with a large bottle of water. What a relief.

When I got back to the apartment I drank 1.5 litres of water and three cups of tea before I started to feel as if I was getting adequately rehydrated. A major lesson learned and if I don't remember it I won't even be finishing the first day of the Marathon des Sables. Also when I got back I found the 10 euro note was in my bag all the time – but in a different pocket! Another lesson, as I also "lost" my contact lenses the same way last year in the Arctic. I know I won't have the need for any money in the Sahara desert, but I do need to make sure I am totally organised and know exactly where everything is in my bag. It is going to be tough enough without making it more of a problem by not being 100% organised.

I recovered enough to do three more runs on Monday, Tuesday and Wednesday before the shock of returning to UK weather. I finished the week off with my long walk day, although did this as a run / walk with 15 minutes of walking followed by 5 minutes of running. I did a total distance of 36 miles, covering most of the Fylde Coast, bringing the week's mileage to 80 miles, as planned, and with the longest walking session complete with rucksack that I have done to date. So despite the hiccups it proved to be a successful week overall.

The next two weeks totalled 77 and 88 miles (the most I have done in one week). The first week of the two was slightly lower than originally planned. On the Sunday after I returned from Tenerife I was staying at my brothers and although I got up at 7am and set off in sub zero temperatures, experiencing difficulty in staying upright as the roads and pavements were so icy, I only had time for 18 miles, before heading off to see my nephew and his family. I had a fairly normal training week with a final run / walk on the Friday. This ended up as 31 miles instead of about 35 which I had planned, but that was because I travelled out to Inglewhite and trained in some more hilly conditions, around Beacon Fell, as I wanted to get the benefit of the ascents and descents in that area which are missing on the very flat Fylde Coast.

The next week went very well and I covered a distance of 88 miles, and ended up with a 36 mile session in 8 and a half hours and carrying 8kgs (17.6lbs). Admittedly I did have a break after about 22 miles when I called in at the surgery where I work. As it was the Friday before Christmas there was the traditional lunch and exchange of presents and I called in for half an hour and had a few sandwiches. The final stage after my lunch break was mainly in rain and with strong winds which are so characteristic of the Fylde coast. I was really pleased with this session, although I could have done with more than 90 minutes to eat, shower and recover before setting off for the work night out!

Christmas week was a low mileage week – not because it was Christmas but because every fourth week I reduce my mileage. I would like to suggest that I had planned for it to coincide with Christmas week – but I am not that organised and it was just a fortunate coincidence. I still did about 30 miles and had a back pack weighing about 7.5kgs (16.5lbs) for all of the runs – and I am glad to say it felt comfortable.

CHAPTER FIVE

TRAINING PHASE 3 – BACK TO BACK SESSIONS

I decided to make some final adjustments for the next 9 or 10 weeks of training before I started to taper. Instead of doing a long session on Friday and a rest day on Sunday I planned to do back to back sessions on Friday and Saturday with a rest day on Sunday. I intended to do a walk / run session on Friday of between 25 miles (if hilly) and a maximum of 40 miles (if on the beach or flat) and 20 to 24 mile runs on Saturday. The back to back runs would help to mimic the reality of the event when I eventually got to the Sahara – minus the heat of course. My weekly mileage over this final three month period is shown in Figure 6.

The year also ended on a reasonably good note in regard to injuries. I did not want to tempt fate but I had been relatively injury free. I had been troubled for the previous two or three months with relatively severe pain in my left foot. At first I was really concerned in case it was the beginning of a stress fracture, which would probably have been the end of my hopes of running in 2009. I kept training without any deterioration and eventually realised I had a Morton's neuroma. This is a swelling of the nerve between two toes giving localised pain and pain into the adjacent two toes. It was very painful if I walked on a hard surface in bare feet and I could feel the swelling between my toes. I decided I would just have to ignore the pain and get on with my training as I was not keen

5 – TRAINING PHASE 3

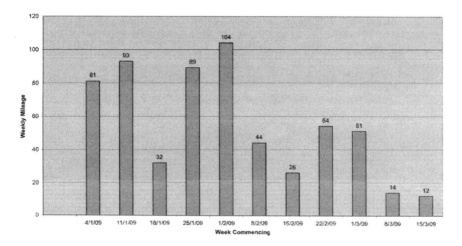

Figure 6   Weekly mileage January 2009 to March 2009

on a steroid injection and again I knew that if I went for surgery I would not be able to recover and do the right amount of training in time for the start of the 2009 Marathon des Sables in March. Fortunately for some reason it started to improve a little over the last two weeks of 2008 and it eventually resolved completely.

As the new year commenced my plan was for a couple of days of hard training on the Friday and Saturday – heading to the Lake District to do part of The Dales Way and get some hills in and a change of scenery on the Friday, and then a beach run on the Saturday. These would be my first high mileage back to back sessions in preparation for the Marathon des Sables. I had last done some back to back sessions, albeit lower mileage, three years previously when training for the Antarctic Marathon. The first session was in the Lake District on The Dales Way. I was in the car and on the way by 7.15am. The temperature was hovering around zero, although much better than New Years Eve. As I got nearer to Crook and the start of the Dales Way I became increasingly reluctant to get out of the warm cocoon of my car into the cold and dark outside. I turned the heater down and my car seat heater off to make it less of a problem!

What a great place to train. Good weather, despite the cold, lovely scenery and challenging terrain to run / walk on. The Dales way is a well marked route, making it very easy for someone like me with no navigation skills. Unfortunately when I got to Burneside the route markers disappeared (well at least I could not see them!) and I ended up doing a detour round Kendal and on to the A6 Shap Road before rejoining The Dales Way. I learned another lesson as having had a look at my map, I decided to keep it out of my bag and set off without remembering to fasten my front pack. A few yards further on and the contents hit the road – my phone and camera fortunately appeared to be able to bounce quite well without any damage!

I turned round after just over 14 miles and thought finding my way back would be easy – just follow the way I came. Towards the end of the session I suddenly realised that I was heading in the wrong direction and appeared to have gone round in a circle and was heading back the way I had set off in the morning! Rather than risk getting it all wrong again I decided to keep to the roads and headed into Crook and then along the main road towards Bowness in the fading light. Fortunately I had my head torch with me so that approaching traffic could see me, as it was dark by the time I reached my car.

I got back to the car after 29 miles in 7.5 hours. I had set off with a backpack weighing 11kgs (about 24lbs) including 3.5 litres of water – so I was probably at the upper limit of what I would be carrying in the Marathon des Sables. My aim was to walk uphill and run the level sections and downhill. I managed to do this apart from some sections where there were sheets of ice and common sense indicated walking was a better option! I was understandably tired but felt OK at the end of the session, and enjoyed a great flask of warm vegetable soup before heading home.

The following morning I would have loved to have stayed in bed – but I won't have that luxury in March, and as I was planning a beach run I had to get off so that I could run before the tide came in. The plan was a 20 mile session on the beach and the aim was to keep running the whole way. I reduced the backpack weight to about 8kgs (17.5lbs). My legs felt very heavy initially but I then got into some sort of rhythm and kept plodding along at a slow pace. I left the car in Lytham and ran to Red

5 – TRAINING PHASE 3

Bank Road in Bispham, which was exactly 10 miles. I turned round and had to keep resisting the temptation to walk – I think if I had stopped running I would not have got going again. I reached South Pier at 14 miles and had the rest of the run broken down in my head into short manageable distances, a good psychological ploy rather than trying to mentally tackle the total distance in one block. However, I had not taken into account the incoming tide. Although there was lots of beach to run on there was a channel right across my path which had filled with water, and so I had the option of wading through cold water 12 inches high or heading back to South Pier and then running along the promenade. A no brainer, although again very tempting to start walking because of the excuse of the extra distance, caused by my detour. As a result I ended up doing 20.7 miles in 4hrs 40mins – a very slow run but very satisfying after the long session the previous day.

So that was 49.7 miles in two days with a total running time of about 12 hours, and I felt really good on the evening of the second run once I had got home and rested for a while. I felt I could happily have gone for another run the following day, but the plan was a rest day and so I was able to look forward to a lie in and a lazy day!

The next week really spurred me on with my training. Although it was slightly lower mileage than planned at about 81miles, it included some good quality sessions and the back to back sessions were slightly shorter but a lot tougher.

On Friday I trained along the Ribble Way Walk. My plan was walking only with a full weight backpack. It was a good job that I had not planned to run as it would have been difficult most of the time. A lot of the way I was walking through thick wet mud in cow and horse churned fields on uneven ground. It was like walking through treacle and the squelching sound as my feet came out of the mud made me think I was about to lose my shoes! As well as this thick treacly mud there were long stretches where there was a superficial layer of mud which made it like an ice skating rink and my feet were sliding in all directions. I will not be taking part in Dancing on Ice as my inelegant performance on the mud would certainly rule me out.

On Saturday I had a training session on the beach which did not work out quite as planned. The first problem setting off from Lytham was an inability to get onto the beach due to sheets of ice – I am not sure I can ever remember seeing so much ice on a beach. I eventually got onto the beach but after just over 8.5 miles the tide had not gone out far enough and I had to either turn round, or else head back onto the promenade. I decided to head back with the intention of doing a few more miles once I got back to the car in order to complete my planned 22 miles for the day. As I turned round it was like walking into a brick wall as the wind was so strong! It was almost as quick to walk as to run and so I decided to conserve some energy and walked most of the way back.

I managed to do about six and a half miles of my eventual 17 miles for the day in sand dunes. I know not as steep or as long as they will be in the Sahara and totally different sand texture – but at least it was better than those taking part who live in the Midlands or London will have on their doorstep. I deliberately picked the steepest and longest sections and at times had to use all fours to get up. I actually quite enjoyed it in some sort of masochistic way as it made a change from same pace running – and on the way back at least the dunes gave me some protection from the wind.

The weather was freezing cold and made worse by the wind. Three years ago to the day I had been in Antarctica waiting for the weather to improve to make it safe to fly out and back to Chile. It was ironic to think that while training for the Sahara I was wearing some of the clothing that I had used when I ran the Ice Marathon! I got back to the car after 17 miles and although I felt OK as far as my legs and general energy levels were concerned I decided, as I was so cold, to call it a day as what I really needed was to get warm, get a hot drink and a good hot shower!

The next week was also high volume at 93 miles and included high quality training with a tempo run and an interval session, as well as two weight sessions in the gym, and it brought me a week closer to the start.

The quality runs were mainly at the beginning of the week and I then had three consecutive high mileage days on Thursday, Friday and Saturday. On Thursday I was exhausted after a 13 mile run despite having planned to do 15 miles. I felt completely drained and was seriously considering a couple of days rest. I was contemplating a glass or two of wine on Thursday night when I decided I would plan for a run and get things ready for an early start – although still not convinced I would be up for it. However I managed to get out and was delighted to do 34.5 miles in eight hours with a pack weighing slightly more than I will be carrying at the start of the Marathon des Sables and probably about 2.5kgs (5.5lbs) more than I will be carrying for the long run.

I was really pleased with my last run of the week. It was a mere 18.5 miles with no back pack and I was running very slowly. It might seem odd to say that I was pleased with such a training session as at that stage in my training it was a relatively short distance run without a pack and at a fairly slow pace. However, the run followed the 34.5 miles of the previous day which I had very nearly backed out of. In addition I only had just over three hours to recover from this long session before heading out to a Sportsman's dinner at my golf club. I did not get back home until nearly 1am and slept badly. I was just about nodding off to sleep when I was disturbed by a text message (my brother Dave had just arrived in Shanghai and seemed to have quickly forgotten that there is a time difference!). I could not get back to sleep as my legs were uncomfortable after the long session that day and eventually I got up at 4am having not slept, and had a cup of tea and a Brufen! So the night mimicked nights in Sahara as I understand sleep is often disturbed due to the discomfort of the ground, strong winds and unstable tents and tent mates snoring (not to mention other of their less desirable bodily noises!).

My alarm was set for 6.45am, and as it was also pitch black I was very tempted to roll over and have a lie in. I am glad that I resisted the temptation as I knew I would be able to look back to these few days when struggling during the Marathon des Sables, as there are bound to be days during the event when I will be tired out and wonder how I will manage a run the following day. And the most encouraging part of the 18.5 mile run was that it felt effortless and at the end I felt I could have carried on, or gone for a further run later that day!

I was looking forward to a much quieter week now as part of my programme of three heavy training weeks and then a lighter week. I was very pleased that I had gone for this approach as it is not only a good way to reduce the risk of injury and illness but it is psychologically important to have a planned lighter week and a chance to ease off.

I rewarded myself for the 3 heavy weeks of training with a Jameson and then some red wine with my take away Indian meal!

The penultimate week of January was an enjoyable low mileage week of running – just over 30 miles and 2 gym sessions. I was about to start my last full, three week high mileage period and after that there was another low mileage week, before building up the mileage again. However this second high mileage period would only be for two weeks – with the second one in Tenerife – as I would then be starting a three week taper which would hopefully see me ready for the start of the Marathon des Sables 2009 which was now only nine weeks away. At this stage I could see the end in sight for my training which was very demanding not only for me in terms of effort and commitment, but also for Cherith as so much of my time of necessity had to be devoted to training.

The dogs, my regular training companions, enjoyed the fact that I had done a low mileage week as they were able to run with me a bit more. Unfortunately Della who has been my running companion for eight years was starting to age and was really not up to anything more than a very short run. BB, as a one year old, was getting old enough to be able to increase the miles without damaging her young bones and soft tissues, so she was taking over, leaving Della a bit long in the face when I set off training.

The final week in January went extremely well although I actually ran a little less in total than planned at 89 miles, although I was still very pleased with this, as total distance although important was not everything. I was particularly pleased with the quality and variety of my training which included gym sessions, tempo runs and interval runs as well as long slow sessions. Again my main effort was on the Friday when I did 26 very hilly miles in the Lake District with a 10kg (22lbs) rucksack, and this was followed by 21 miles running on Saturday.

5 – TRAINING PHASE 3

On Friday morning the alarm was going off at 6.15am. It was pitch black, the wind was howling around the house and it was pouring down with rain! The delights of training! By the time I got to Coniston, at 8.30am, it was raining in a way that it can only do in the Lake District. I was very tempted to stay in the car but stepped out and pulled on full waterproofs before setting off on the Cumbria Way. By the time I had been going for an hour my gloves could quite literally be rung out. My route took me via Tarn Howes and Colwith Force to Skelwith Bridge and then via Elterwater and Chapel Stile to Dungeon Ghyll, my turn around point. I was going well so that before returning back by the same route I set off up the track at the back of Dungeon Ghyll heading towards Stickle Tarn. It took me over 30 minutes to do the next 0.6 miles as it was very steep and very slippery with all the rain. I climbed about 900 feet during this time. (I did not realise at the time how useful this would be psychologically when I had to tackle something very similar after 32 miles on the long day in the Sahara, and I was able to remind myself that I could handle this sort of terrain.) I did not make it to Stickle Tarn as I was concerned about doing the return journey in time before it got dark. I got back to my car just before 5pm, having had a few hours with very little rain. However, just as I got back it started to pour down again and so my "dry clothes" which I changed into for the journey back were soaked through by the time I was ready to get back into the car.

Despite the exertion of Friday I also managed a slow 21 mile run the following day and I felt fine at the end. I felt I must be getting it right in time for the Marathon des Sables, now only eight weeks away – and I was counting the days down.

My full training week was as follows:

SUNDAY   Gym – 10 minutes on bike followed by a weights session

MONDAY   7a.m. – 5 miles slow – 46mins 33secs
            1p.m. – 8 miles tempo – 2 miles warm up and warm down with 4 miles in 31.15 (average 7.49 per mile)

TUESDAY	Gym – 10 minutes bike followed by weights session
WEDNESDAY	7a.m. – 5 miles slow – 48mins 46secs
	4p.m. – 9 miles interval – 2 miles warm up and down with 4 miles intervals and 1/2 mile recovery jog (mile times 7.40; 7.33; 7.33 and 7.55)
THURSDAY	12.30p.m. – 15 miles slow in 2 hours 37mins 21secs (average 10.25 per mile)
FRIDAY	8.45a.m. – 26 miles with 7,500 feet elevation in 7 hours 55 minutes
SATURDAY	11.30a.m. – 21 miles slow – 4 hours 10 minutes (average 12 minutes per mile)

At the beginning of February while most of the country had been brought to a standstill by unprecedented amounts of snow, and training for many of those running in the Marathon des Sables had been seriously curtailed, as usual hardly any snow had fallen in Blackpool and my training was able to continue unaltered. In fact apart from an odd flurry and a superficial covering lasting for a few hours only, we were snow free and the last two days of my training week had seen clear blue skies and lots of sunshine.

The training followed a similar pattern to the previous week. The intention had been to head to the Lakes again on the Friday but in view of the weather and the resultant tragic deaths of two climbers I decided to use some common sense. I changed my plans to two long local training sessions. The intention was to spend about 10 hours on the go on Friday with a full rucksack and to cover probably about 40 miles while leaving enough energy in the tank for an 8 hour session on Saturday covering about 30 miles.

I set off about 7.30am on Friday and went via Weeton, Plumpton, Westby and Ballam to the front at Lytham. I then turned and headed north along the beach for about 14 miles until I got to Rossall. Unfortunately while I was heading off the beach I had to walk through a lot of water which was deeper than I realised. Even my excellent waterproof shoes could not cope when the water was past my ankles.

5 – TRAINING PHASE 3

My feet were soaking and I had to stop and change my socks (which I could wring out) for a dry pair from my bag. My shoes were wet through and I was concerned about blisters, but I had no need to worry as no blisters had developed even after two hard days of training. I headed back along the River Wyre where I saw a moored boat which I am sure was aptly named "Good Hope" at one stage, but the dreams had now turned into a wreck. I hoped that it was not some sort of omen! I returned home via Poulton and then finished off by taking the dogs for a four mile walk.

I was walking / running for 9 hours and 57 minutes and covered 38.5 miles. It was a slower average pace than I had expected. However, when I got home I thought my bag was rather heavy and so I weighed it. I had obviously made a mistake before setting off, when I had thought that my bag was lighter than I had planned and so I had added another 2kg (4.4lbs) weight from my gym. However, the actual weight when I set off, with water, must have been about 13kgs (28.5lbs). As I expect to be carrying no more than 11.5kgs (just over 25lbs) with water on day 1, and as this will drop to about 9.5kgs (30lbs) by the time of the 50 mile day, I was obviously training with a heavier rucksack than I will be carrying. So I actually felt very pleased.

So I had achieved two of my training aims – a long day on my feet covering a long distance with a full rucksack but the question still remained as to whether the third intended outcome was to be achieved – that is to be able to do another long day the next day. Again, I was delighted that I was able to do 30.2 miles in 7 hours 32 minutes. My bag weight was reduced to about 8kgs (17.5lbs), and I felt really good at the end, and had recovered well by the following day, and as I had noted previously I felt I could do it all again, so my training was still well on course.

I ended the week having done the highest mileage at 105 miles that I would be doing in my training, and the highest mileage I have ever done in one week. Although I would still be doing high mileage for another three to four weeks the plan was to reduce my weekly mileage and concentrate on quality sessions (tempo and intervals) along with gym sessions. The back to back sessions of the previous week had confirmed my training was on course and had been psychologically important, but I did not feel I would gain anything by more similar sessions at this stage – apart from an unwanted injury.

CHAPTER FIVE

TRAINING PHASE 4 – TAPERING AND THE HEAT CHAMBER

I started this final phase of my training with a tempo session on the Monday, covering a total distance of eight miles, and followed it with an interval session on the Wednesday of 9 miles. I was encouraged that my mile split times were quicker than during previous similar sessions. I also managed two gym sessions. On the Thursday my planned mileage was curtailed as I spent a considerable time in the afternoon in the garage as for the second time in two weeks I had a flat tyre on my car. As the tyres are the "run flat" type of tyres this also meant a second bill in two weeks of £270.

This was possibly a good thing (the reduced mileage not the bill), as I had been very tired at the end of this week.

I really struggled on both the Friday and the Saturday. I went to the Lake District again on Friday and had a much nicer day. I did just over 21 miles with a full rucksack with lots of hills to tackle, which was what I was looking for. However, I struggled and felt very tired at the end. I was going to do a training session of 15 to 20 miles in the sand dunes on Saturday, but wimped out when I saw the rain. Instead I did a treadmill session in the gym, with a gradually increasing gradient each mile, but stopped after eight miles as I felt drained. I felt very tired and generally aching by Saturday night. Cherith had some sort of viral infection so I was not sure if I had also picked something up or was just tired from the high mileage and high intensity training that I had been doing over a number of weeks.

Fortunately after many years of running I know my body fairly well and I also knew that a few days of reduced mileage or complete rest would not make any difference. On the following day I felt a bit better and was starting a "quiet week" in which I planned to do no more than 30 to 40 miles. Following that I knew that ten days in the following two weeks would be in Tenerife, with some warmer weather and a change of scenery and lots of recovery time lazing round the pool with a book or two. Then I would be tapering for the final three weeks, so I felt as if training was coming to an end.

I enjoyed a very gentle recovery week – I did just less than 30 miles and also managed three gym sessions and three core muscle sessions. I also actually played golf for the first time in about six months as well as getting out with my camera for a couple of hours. It made a good change from churning out the miles.

On 24th February I received some good news for my final training plans. I had my phone call returned from one of the lecturers at Liverpool John Moore University confirming that I would be able to use their environment chamber before setting off for the Sahara. I had contacted them the previous week and was not sure if it would be possible to use their heat chamber to help with acclimatisation before setting off. The call that I received was from Ben Edwards, an environmental physiologist – but even better he had done the Marathon des Sables himself in 2005, so had real practical experience of what I would be facing. (By coincidence his finishing position and my race number happened to be exactly the same.)

The plan was for four sessions (March 11th, 13th, 18th and 20th) wearing the same kit as I would be running in and carrying my rucksack and taking fluids on board as expected for the event. The temperature was to be between 30 and 35°C and I would do one hour sessions. This

6 – TRAINING PHASE 4

would push up my core temperature and should help me to acclimatise to the temperatures I would face in the Marathon des Sables. I would also have my weight checked before and after each run and would monitor my pulse rate and this would give me a good idea about fluid replacement strategies. As well as the physical benefits I was expecting it would help me psychologically to experience the expected temperatures that I would face during the event.

I started the final phase of high mileage weeks with a 10 mile sand dune run on the Sunday. I had eventually decided to take trekking poles with me to the Sahara and used them for this training session – what a difference they made when working my way up and down the steeper sand dunes. I followed up with an eight mile run Monday lunchtime with the middle four as a tempo run and then had a gym session for an hour on Tuesday and nine miles intervals on Wednesday, before heading to the airport and out to the apartment in Tenerife on the Thursday. I was again looking forward to running in some warmer weather – predicted to be low 20s on the Friday and Saturday – and hopefully this would also help a little with acclimatising.

Well in comparison with the rain, wind, hail and snow at home I guess it was warm, although not as warm as I had been hoping for. However, I still managed to get some good training in which I hoped would help a bit with adapting to the heat in Sahara.

I had a gentle nine mile run on the first day without carrying a bag with me. I followed this with two days back to back running of 20 miles each day and carrying about 9kgs (20lbs). On the first day it was quite warm and the temperature outside the pharmacy as I went through Las Galletas was 25°C. I think that was as hot as it got. Both days went well and I did not feel as if they had taken anything out of me and that I could have done it all again for a third day. In addition I got in two quality runs – a five mile tempo session in sub eight minute pace and eight half mile intervals all at about 3 minutes 45 seconds pace. My total for the week was just over 50 miles and I also got in one gym session in Las Galletas and three sessions of core muscle training.

On the Wednesday after I returned, I had my first session in the heat chamber at Liverpool University. They forgot to tell me until the last email that they would be constantly monitoring my core temperature while in the chamber and pull me out if it went above 39°C. I will leave it to your imagination which orifice they used to monitor my temperature – but it is below my neck! I felt that if I could survive that I could survive anything that the Sahara threw at me!

The first session was at a modest 31°C and I was carrying about 7kgs (15.5lbs), and the second session on the Friday was with the temperature cranked up to 38°C and carrying nearer 10kgs (22lbs). I did 40 minutes on the treadmill on both days and my aim was to keep my pulse at my endurance level – between 130 and 140. I managed to do that fairly well and did around 3 miles each day. The sessions were an interesting experience and also, hopefully, physically and psychologically helpful.

I had been advised that I would have to stop if my core temp reached 39.5°C. On the first session (and also in fact on the subsequent sessions) that did not happen, although it was not possible to be absolutely sure during the run as the probe fell out (thank God!). However I checked my core temperature at the end of session and it had only gone up very slightly to 38.3°C. The other good feature was that my weight at the end of the run was exactly the same as at the start, so although I was sweating a lot I was also managing to replace my fluids adequately.

As well as the above sessions I did some light training totalling about 25 miles in total for the week as part of my tapering down, plus a few weight and core muscle sessions. The idea at this stage was to keep ticking over but also to realise that the training had been done and I needed to make sure that I was fresh and injury free ready for the start of the 24th Marathon des Sables.

In the week before my departure I had my final two sessions in the heat chamber. The third session saw the temperature increased to about 40°C and then finally to 43°C at the maximum. I did 50 minute sessions and did just over 3 miles each time. I had packed my rucksack with everything I would be taking with me – somehow it all goes in – so it was a good test mimicking as far as possible what I would face when I got out there.

6 – TRAINING PHASE 4

And so at long last my training was completed. I was not planning anything more than a few walks during the final few days before leaving the UK. I felt that I had planned my training in a way that was just right for me and that I had stuck to my training plans meticulously, despite the weather and other potential setbacks, and had come through injury free, fitter than I had probably ever been and hopefully ready for "the toughest footrace on earth".

PART THREE

PLANNING
AND
PREPARATION

CHAPTER SEVEN

ESSENTIAL EQUIPMENT, MEDICAL KIT AND HYGINE

The Marathon des Sables is a self-sufficiency event. This means that all competitors have to carry everything that they need for the whole week in a rucksack on their back. The only items provided by the organisers are a Berber tent and water, which is provided at the start and end of each day and at check-points, positioned approximately every 6 miles.

The rules and regulations state that the rucksack must weigh between 6.5kgs (14.3lbs) and 15kgs (33lbs) – (Rule 24). I have no idea why there is a maximum weight, and indeed one of my tent mates exceeded it considerably with a rucksack weighing almost 18kgs (nearly 40lbs). This weight does not include the daily water supply which consists of 1.5 litres provided at the start of each day and at most checkpoints, with 3 litres at the other checkpoints. In addition 4.5 litres is provided at the end of each day to be used for rehydration, cooking and washing. The total rucksack weight will increase therefore by 1.5kgs (3.3lbs) to 3kgs (6.6lbs) at the start of each day and at the various check-points. Obviously as the race proceeds and food is consumed the pack weight decreases.

My personal aim was to have a total weight, before water, of less than 11kgs (24lbs). A balance had to be struck between keeping the weight down, as additional weight will mean a slower pace and longer on the trail with less time to recover, and making sure I had everything I needed and that what I had with me was fit for purpose. It is possible to have a sleeping bag, for example, which is extremely lightweight but it may not be adequate in terms of its minimum temperature for cold nights in the desert. Another important factor was that the high quality, lightweight equipment was in many cases considerably more expensive than slightly heavier weight items.

In planning my equipment strategy I was helped by Martin from Likeys (www.likeys.com) who gave excellent unbiased advice, not only to me but also to many other competitors. I also became a regular visitor to www.themds.co.uk. This web site, developed by Mike Adams, was an invaluable source of information and advice, with veterans of the event sharing their experience with 2009 competitors and a regular cross fertilisation of ideas. The information in the site had to be taken with some degree of caution, particularly in the section about illness and injuries and that on training, as many people offered well intended advice which in my opinion, based on many years of training and my medical knowledge, was not always accurate.

I first seriously started my planning in early January 2008 when I attended a one day seminar in London organised by Luke Cunliffe, a previous contestant. I travelled to London on the Saturday afternoon, having already booked a hotel, which I believed was close to the pub where the seminar was to be held the next day. That was my first mistake as I had actually booked a hotel several miles away. I got completely lost trying to find where I was meant to be staying. I had one major concern about the event and that was navigation, particularly on the long overnight stage. This was not a good omen. If I could not find a hotel in London what were my chances of successfully negotiating the dunes and trails of the Sahara in the dark?

The seminar was very useful and I would recommend it or one of the other similar events that are available to future contestants. The value was not just in the factual information provided but also in starting to focus my attention at an early stage on what was required. I was determined that there would be no last minute panicking and that I would have my kit and food sorted with a minimum of four weeks to go before the event.

The first item I bought was my rucksack. There are a number of options here, as with most of the remainder of the kit. I opted for the Raidlight 30 litre rucksack. This is a bag that has been well trialled by previous entrants and at 30 litres capacity I expected that it would be large enough to get all my kit in. I was determined that I would not be carrying sleeping bags, a thermarest and other equipment on the outside. I could not see the point of going for a 25 litre bag as some did and then carrying a shed load of equipment on the outside.

Putting the bag together was a job in itself, particularly as the information provided was in French. The bag has a front waist pack which I used to carry items I needed for each day. Attaching this pack and more specifically attaching it so that it did not bounce up and down took quite a lot of time and patience. I also used the shoulder strap bottle carriers and again it took some perseverance firstly to attach them to the rucksack and then to clip the rucksack together when the bottles were in position. The final problem was finding the whistle. A whistle is a compulsory item of equipment. I did not know it when I bought my Raidlight rucksack but a whistle is incorporated into the pack. It was only when I visited the MDS web site that I found reference to this whistle, and even then it took me a long time to find it. Nobody has actually managed to beat my bet and find the whistle without advice.

ESSENTIAL EQUIPMENT

Rule 24 as well as advising the weight of equipment also stipulates certain items of equipment which every competitor has to carry and which theoretically can be checked by the organisers at any stage of the race, with time penalties imposed if any items are missing. I did not hear of this being carried out at any stage. The equipment is as follows:

- backpack or equivalent (best suited to each participant),

- sleeping bag
- torch with spare batteries
- 10 safety pins
- compass, with 1° or 2° precision
- lighter
- a whistle
- knife with metal blade
- tropical disinfectant
- anti-venom pump
- a signalling mirror
- one aluminium survival sheet.

The "tropical disinfectant" is actually a reflection of the fact that the rules are written in French and translated and should read "topical disinfectant". I took some iodine with me and as the rules do not stipulate the amount I took a very small volume from work, along with some cotton wool buds. These were so that I could apply small amounts to any sores or blisters without spilling and wasting it by pouring it directly out of a bottle. I also assumed that if I really needed any significant treatment that I would be able to get that from the medical team and that I would abide by the letter of the law and while taking topical disinfectant, take only a minimum amount.

The other item which gave amusement to many of my friends was the anti-venom pump. This consists of a small nozzle which is applied to the skin over any insect or snake bites and a syringe which is then attached to suck the bite out of the skin. I am not aware that this has ever been used in the 24 years of the Marathon des Sables. The pump did however prove to be extremely useful. I wanted to take some gaffer tape with me in case of any immediately necessary repairs to my rucksack or shoes or gaiters. I could only find large rolls which weighed about 100g. I removed a small amount from the roll and wrapped it around the syringe of the anti-venom pump. The pump, in this way, served a dual purpose. Not my original idea, but lateral thinking is essential in planning for the Marathon des Sables.

There are a number of sleeping bags which would have served my purpose. I tend to feel the cold and so wanted to make sure that I had an adequate bag. I opted for the PHD minimus bag with 900 down, which is stated to be able to cope with a temperature of 5°C. I also took a silk liner to sleep in, which is placed inside the sleeping bag and combined with the bag would provide a comfort temperature of zero. In practice I could have managed without the liner. The advantage of the bag and liner was that they compressed together and took up minimal space.

The value of planning was demonstrated to me when I noticed another competitor whose sleeping bag weighed 1.6kgs (3.5lbs). That was almost the same weight as the total weight of my sleeping bag and thermarest as well as clothing for night-time and running the long stage overnight and a pair of flip flops for use around the camp site.

The one mistake that I made in relationship to equipment was with my head torch. I opted for the Petzl e+LITE as it weighed only 34g including the spare batteries. This head torch is really designed as an emergency back-up torch and proved to be woefully inadequate on the overnight phase of the long stage. This mistake was an example of trying to reduce weight but at the expense of functionality.

I opted for the Victorinox Swiss Card from the makers of the well known Swiss knife. This amazing piece of equipment is about the size of a credit card, weighs a mere 25g (less than one ounce), but includes a knife, scissors, file, tooth pick and a variety of other tools (none of which were needed apart from the knife and scissors).

The whistle was included in my rucksack, and with the purchase of a Silva Expedition 4 Compass I only needed to obtain the other few essential items, which can readily be obtained via the internet from a wide variety of sources. Again I searched around to get the lowest weight items possible.

MEDICAL AND HYGINE

It might be thought that as a doctor I would have no problem in deciding on my medical kit and that I would head out to the Sahara fully equipped. I actually hate taking medication – perhaps I have seen the harm it can do!

I wanted to keep my rucksack weight down and I assumed that the official medical team would have everything I needed. I decided to take with me a limited amount of drugs and dressings for use in case of emergency, for example if I needed to sort out a problem while out on the trail and between check-points.

I obviously needed to sort out my vaccinations. I added to those that most people would have a cholera vaccine. This may sound odd as there was no risk of cholera. There is, however, some evidence that the cholera vaccine offers a degree of protection against traveller's diarrhoea. I estimated from the available evidence that ten people would have to take the vaccine to avoid one case of traveller's diarrhoea. As the side effects from the vaccine are minimal and as the consequences of developing diarrhoea in this situation were potentially very serious, I decided that the benefits outweighed any possible risk. It is of course impossible to know if I would have developed diarrhoea if I had not had the vaccine.

After I had taken part in the High Peak 40 I developed a horrible blister on my heel. I used a Mepilex border lite dressing. I found this was very comfortable, stayed in place and was not bulky so that I had no problems getting my trainers on while using it. I opted to take just a few of these in different sizes. I am not a great believer in too much interference in any treatment areas and specifically when it comes to blisters think that more harm is done by interfering than by leaving alone. I refused to take scalpel blades and the other paraphernalia that others were considering, but instead opted for a few needles in case I had a tense blister and needed to make a hole to drain off any fluid.

As far as medication was concerned I took a few painkillers, tablets for sickness and diarrhoea and an antibiotic in case of traveller's diarrhoea. A number of people took ibuprofen or in some cases stronger anti-inflammatory drugs which had been prescribed for them. There are some real concerns about the risk of acute renal failure when taking these drugs if dehydrated and as I was likely to need pain relief and not reduce inflammation, I decided to just take Paracetamol. I was surprised to find that some people had taken much stronger pain killers with them, such as Tramadol, even though they had not tried them out before. In my experience a lot of people get some severe reactions to these stronger pain killers. I did not think it was a good idea to find out that they caused drowsiness, vomiting, confusion or other problems when competing in such adverse circumstances. The only desirable side effect for most people would have been the all too common constipation that they cause!

In case of any gut problems I took a few tablets of Buccastem. These would be useful if I was vomiting, particularly as they dissolve in the mouth and so I would be able to keep them down even if I was being sick. Like most people I also took Imodium in readiness for any bouts of diarrhoea. In addition I took with me Ciprofloxacin. This antibiotic is of value in traveller's diarrhoea. The only concern was its side effect of tendon problems and potentially tendon rupture. However, as this is more common in the elderly and those on steroids and the risk is less than 1 in 10,000 I decided that I would use it if I developed diarrhoea with the potential risk that this would itself prevent me from completing the event.

Personal hygiene was always going to be an issue, and obviously far from ideal. That was no excuse for not at least trying to maintain standards, particularly in relationship to hand hygiene and handling of food. I took in my kit some soap leaves which can be used for personal washing as well as washing clothes and mugs. In addition for my own hygiene purposes I took Wet Wipes and at the last minute put a small bottle of alcohol hand gel in my kit. I would never do this or a similar event without taking this with me. I used it at every possible opportunity and I believe it played a significant role in keeping me free from the vomiting and diarrhoea bug which hit about two out of every three of the UK competitors.

I packed the smallest tooth brush I could find with a minimal amount of toothpaste. It goes without saying that toilet paper was required – but how much? I guessed and I guessed right but I hate to think what would have happened with a bad case of diarrhoea. The Tyvek paper suit may have had a dual role, as it did for one competitor.

Finally I needed sun cream – P20 – and a lip balm. Essential items and well used after the first few days.

CHAPTER EIGHT

SHOES, SOCKS AND GAITERS

The most critical items of equipment are shoes, socks and gaiters. Attempting to avoid trashing your feet is essential and having been happy with my training and physical preparation my only concerns about my ability to finish the event related to my feet and / or illness or injury. It surprised me to find that some people were still making decisions about which socks to use a matter of two weeks before the event, while others had not used their shoes until the event and others were still sorting out how to attach gaiters over the few days leading up to the start.

I have odd feet. Not just odd in terms of different sized feet but a very broad foot, a bony prominence on the outside of my foot, a heel bone which sticks out and toes which are a bit flexed. I have problems getting comfortable shoes, my socks never feel particularly comfortable and over the years I have had some blisters on my toes and heels. I also overpronate (a technical term which means my foot doesn't hit the ground properly) and use orthotics. For me getting this combination of shoes, socks and gaiters right was critical.

I had been running in 2007 and the first half of 2008 in Mizuno Wave Rider shoes and they appeared to suit me. I was not sure whether to use ordinary running shoes or trail shoes. I tried a pair of trail shoes made by Innov-8 and the first pair seemed OK, but then I found the second pair was causing blisters – so back to the drawing board. I had plenty of opportunity to try a number of different shoes because with the mileage I was doing and the need to change shoes approximately every 400 miles to avoid injury I was going through a pair every four to six weeks.

In late October 2008, I saw a pair of shoes reviewed in Runner's World magazine. They were the PT-03 Desert shoe made by UK Gear. This company only manufactures shoes after they have been trialled by the British Army. This particular model of shoe was designed as the name implies for use in the desert and had been tested in Afghanistan. It seemed as though this may be the answer to my requirements.

I bought a pair and shortly after headed out to Tenerife. This seemed the ideal place to test them out as I would be running in warmer weather, on volcanic trails and with a lot of dust and small stones, which could get inside my shoes.

The result – for me this was the ideal shoe. I spent two weeks running in Tenerife with temperatures up to 30°C, running on dusty, sandy tracks littered with volcanic rocks. They were the best pair of shoes I had ever run in. Very comfortable, great support and despite running 150 miles in the two weeks I had absolutely no problems. Normally when I use a new shoe I will break it in, alternating the new one with my older shoe. I did not bother with these new shoes, as they were so impressive and I never felt they would cause a problem by using them all the time

I got back and bought the gaiters which are made by the same manufacturer for use with this shoe, and planned to try them out on the sand dunes near Blackpool. Incidentally, when I first used the PT-03 desert shoe in the warm weather of Tenerife I had run in my normal size shoes and despite my feet swelling to some degree still had no problems, so I was not sure what size I would order. Many people suggest a pair of shoes two sizes bigger than normal in order to accommodate any foot swelling which may occur in the heat and with being on the go for so long each day and also to accommodate any taping that may be required.

I believe this is wrong advice and eventually opted for a pair of shoes ½ a size bigger than normal. I believe that a lot of people get blisters because they follow the advice to go two sizes bigger and then

8 – SHOES, SOCKS AND GAITERS

find their feet are rolling around loosely inside their shoes at the start of the event. I also rationalised that if I had problems with my feet swelling or excessive taping I could reduce from two pairs of socks to one, remove my insoles and as a last resort remove my orthotics. My decision was justified as I had no problems with my feet at any stage. It would be interesting to know if it would have been the same if the temperature had been at the normal level rather than the somewhat cooler temperatures I experienced.

I had to take into account that this particular shoe cost £100 (now increased to £110) but if my feet did not hold up I would potentially not be finishing and then all the cost of getting there and the other equipment would have been wasted, so it seemed a worthwhile investment.

As mentioned in the training section of this book, UK Gear also makes a PT-03 Winter shoe. This shoe is the same basic design as the desert shoe but is adapted for the UK winter with a waterproof guarantee, and I did not get my feet wet once despite the awful winter weather I trained in and walking through large pools of water on Blackpool beach. I started to use them towards the end of November and initially tried them for a 32 mile long walk when they caused a bit of havoc with my feet. I am not sure why, apart from the possibility that I was wearing thicker socks than when I was running in hotter weather in Tenerife.

For me this pair of shoes was exactly what I needed. I know some people used the shoes and had problems. No one pair of shoes is suitable for everyone. I was, however, impressed on my return to receive a phone call from UK Gear asking how I had got on with their shoes and discussing their plans to adapt and improve them on the basis of feedback that they were receiving.

I think over the years I have tried every type of sock made by every manufacturer, without finding the ideal sock for my misshapen feet. I remember visiting one web site and ordering six different types of socks, even including tennis socks. On 1st January 2009 I wrote in my blog "have still to make final decision about which socks to run in."

It was about this time I decided to experiment with Toe-toe socks. As the name implies these socks are designed to accommodate the toes separately in the same way as a pair of gloves. There are numerous claims for them and I decided to give them a try.

When I first used them the main problem was actually getting them onto my feet and getting each toe in separately. It is not like slipping on a pair of gloves. I wondered how on earth I would manage sitting on the floor in the desert, and particularly how easy it would be if my toes were taped up. I almost gave up after using them just a couple of times, but fortunately I persevered. I am so glad I stuck with them because after a short while I got used to putting them on, although never as easy as a normal pair of socks, and once they were on my feet they felt incredibly comfortable. I had made yet another decision.

When I ran in the Inaugural Antarctic Ice Marathon I had used two pairs of silk socks, and then two pairs of wool socks. One reason for this was obviously to keep my feet warm. There was also a second reason for the silk socks. This was because it would be better to have friction between two layers of socks rather than between my socks and my feet. I opted for the same concept and on the advice of Martin from Likeys I used a pair of Bridgedale X-Hale multisports as my outer sock. The manufacturers state "when it's hot these socks exhale the heat, keeping your feet cool, particularly in extreme heat and during exercise". I have no idea if there is any scientific basis for this claim but two unwashed pairs of Toe-toes and one pair of Bridgedale X-Hale socks were enough to get me round the Marathon des Sables free of blisters.

I had sorted out shoes, which were sand proof, and two pairs of socks but I was still not happy that sand would not get into my shoes and act as a skin irritant and cause blisters. Most runners in the Marathon des Sables use gaiters and I felt that this was a necessary addition to my footwear.

There are numerous types of gaiters available and many different ways of attaching them. This implied to me that there was no ideal approach. I had used the gaiters, which are specifically designed by UK Gear to be used with their desert shoes, on the beach and in the sand dunes at St Annes and Blackpool. Although they had been completely effective I decided not to use these. This was based on advice that I had

8 – SHOES, SOCKS AND GAITERS

received that the sand texture would be very different in the Sahara and that they may not be effective in that situation. The advice not to use these gaiters was correct, but for the wrong reason. Those who used UK Gear long gaiters did not get any sand in their shoes. There was, however, an unforeseen zip failure and large amounts of gaffer tape were needed to hold the gaiter together. (UK Gear has been made aware of this problem and has identified the cause and is already working to resolve the problem.)

I had decided against UK Gear gaiters but there were still a lot to choose from. I read through a number of blogs of previous competitors as well as the MDS forum and was able to exclude quite a number, which had obviously not turned out to be fit for purpose. By a process of elimination I decided to go for those made by Sandbaggers. The Sandbaggers team are expedition and race organisers and based on their personal experience they have designed gaiters, but I still had a choice as they had two designs. I opted for the smaller one and not only because they were made out of a fetching tangerine colour, the same colour as Blackpool FC play in. On their website they provide the following information and make a very brave claim. "Our silk sand gaiters are based on a tried and tested design which has been a firm favourite with desert runners for many years. Made from ripstop nylon (aka. Parachute silk) …the gaiters are durable, comfortable and, most importantly 100% effective at keeping sand out of your footwear. We have supplied more than half of this year's UK MdS entrants with these gaiters".

This seemed good enough for me and a pair of size 12s were ordered. The gaiters have an elastic band that fits tightly above the ankle and the lower part of the gaiter has Velcro on the inside. This strip of Velcro is then securely fixed to a second strip of Velcro attached to the shoe.

There are numerous ideas about how to secure the lower part of the gaiter to the shoe. Some people use a very basic approach and apply gaffer tape around the gaiter and shoe. I wanted to opt for something more secure. The options appeared to be to attach the Velcro to the shoe by gluing, sewing or a combination of gluing and sewing. I opted for the belt and braces approach and also decided this was not a job for a ham fisted DIYer, but needed a professional.

I wanted to break in the specific pair of shoes that I would be running in when I was in Tenerife in early March and I did not want the Velcro attached at that stage with the risk that it would get scuffed and damaged before I even started the Marathon des Sables. I only had just over two weeks, however, from when I returned from Tenerife before I set off to travel to Morocco. Not wanting to take any chances I visited Timpsons in my local Tesco. Timpsons web site has a strap line – "great service by great people". If only!

I called in before going to Tenerife and explained my requirements. The "great person" I spoke to was absolutely confident that there would be no problem in sorting out what I needed. I went on holiday in a relaxed frame of mind – the last task had been resolved. On my return on the Sunday I called in again with the shoes and the Velcro and left them with the local manager, who advised that the person who would do them was off duty that day.

I phoned back the next day and should have realised that all was not going to be plain sailing. I spoke to a different person who was very apprehensive and expressed concern about the glue holding in the temperatures we were likely to experience. He also explained that it would not be possible to stitch the whole way round the base of the shoe. As I already appreciated that this would not be possible this did not cause any concern. I phoned a cobbler in Yorkshire who I knew had done a good job for some other entrants and got details about the glue that they used. I relayed this information back to Timpsons and thought the problem was resolved.

Three days later, and having heard nothing, I phoned to check progress. Horror of horrors – nothing had happened. Well actually that is not quite true. The shoes had been sent to another branch about eight miles away where there was "a more experienced" cobbler. Nice of them to let me know. I phoned up immediately to find that nothing had happened and that the more experienced cobbler was not working that day either. I asked them to phone the cobbler in Yorkshire and when I

8 – SHOES, SOCKS AND GAITERS

spoke again later they were happy that they knew exactly what needed to be done and that my shoes would be ready to collect after 4.30pm the following day from the store where I had initially left them.

On my way back from my second session in the heat chamber I popped in to pick them up. The young man who had done the job wore a look of pride as he presented my shoes to me with the gaiters attached and from a distance looking very secure. All was well – until he explained that he had not been able to sew the Velcro around the whole of the shoe and had therefore taken a decision to attach and glue the Velcro in sections only at those sites where he could also stitch them. This meant that the gaiter was only attached at certain points with large intermediate gaps which would allow as much sand as possible to get inside the gaiter, and therefore potentially into my shoes.

Although this may come as a surprise to those who know me well, I somehow managed to stay reasonably calm. I pointed out that the job was not only a complete waste of time but that it had potentially messed up the shoes as I now had strips of Velcro inappropriately attached and making it difficult for myself or someone else to do a proper job. "Great service by great people" meant that I was told that I was not going to be charged. I think they may have had extreme difficulty in extracting any money from me.

I had spent many hours over many months making sure that everything was meticulously organised. Now at the last minute I was being let down by the incompetence of somebody else. I contacted the company in Yorkshire who I had spoken to for advice. I should have contacted them at the beginning of the week when I was first aware of a problem. I had been apprehensive about putting my shoes in the post and waiting for them to come back so close to the event. I did not need to have any concerns. The shoes were parcelled up on Monday lunchtime and were back with me by Thursday lunchtime. A thoroughly professional job had been done with the Velcro securely glued the whole way round the base of the shoe and stitched firmly into place. I will always be grateful to Cobblers and Keys (Barnsley Road, South Elmsall, West Yorkshire. 01977 644738).

My feet were sorted and as I was to discover the effort was worthwhile. The combination of two pairs of socks, UK Gear PT-03 Desert shoes and Sandbaggers gaiters secured via glue and stitching was ideal for me. I had no problems with my feet at any stage and at the end of each day I shook out my shoes and not a grain of sand came out. Sandbaggers very brave promise was a reality.

CHAPTER NINE

RUNNING IN THE NUDE – JUST SUNGLASSES

On 23rd January 2009 I posted my kit list on the MDS forums web site to ask for any comments as I wanted to check and see if I had got everything right. Within 22 minutes I received a reply "are you running naked?"

I had not intended to include in the kit list the clothes that I would be running in, as these would obviously not be adding to the weight of my rucksack. By mistake, however, I had forgotten to include in the list the clothes that I would need for the long stage when I would be running overnight and also that I would need around the camp site and at night when the temperature dropped potentially to 5°C. I quickly pointed out that running naked would not be a pretty sight and amended my kit list.

I had a wide range of clothes to consider for competing in. Some people opt for T-shirts and shorts and some swear by long sleeved tops and compression tights, with various combinations of all of these being proposed. I decided to go for the Under-Armour T-shirt and shorts. The shirt was the Under Armour 'Euro' II Metal Loose T Crew. This is described by the company as a shirt that "brings the ultimate in moisture transfer and heat dispersion to your workout... it quickly moves moisture away from the skin and to the outside surface keeping you dry... ensures ventilation where you need it most... to prevent chafing. Recommended for Training in the hottest conditions."

I also opted for the Under Armour Long Compression Short.

I have no idea again about the scientific basis for these claims – although they sound very impressive. In reality the most important factor for me was that they felt comfortable and did not cause any chafing. They appeared to do the job in terms of wicking moisture away from my skin, although I am sure that many other shirts and shorts would have been equally effective.

A lot of people spent a lot of time worrying about what to wear. I am not convinced it makes a lot of difference. I think any technical shirts or shorts are more than appropriate and at the end of the day it comes down to individual preference about which manufacturers' products feel comfortable for each individual and again personal preference is what matters most in deciding whether to use shorts and T-shirts or long sleeved tops and trousers.

Head protection is obviously important in the heat and sunshine and I opted for a Marmot sunhat with an integral neck cape. The protection for my neck seemed a sensible option.

Not only did I have to plan the clothing that I would run in, but I also had to give some thought to what I would wear overnight during the long stage and wear during the evening and overnight at the camp. The temperature in the Sahara at that time of year can drop to between 5 and 10°C. This may not seem particularly cold but in practice it feels a lot colder if the daytime temperatures have been in the mid 30s or even higher. This is aggravated by the fact that I would have been exerting myself in these higher temperatures and then resting and cooling down during the evening.

Again the aim was to have lightweight clothing which would be effective. Many competitors use lightweight paper suits such as those produced by Tyvek. These suits are very familiar to most people being the type of suits worn by Crime Scene Investigators. They are very light (mine weighed a mere 185g – six ounces), crumple up to a very small size and are said to keep you extremely warm.

9 – RUNNING IN THE NUDE

I chose the two piece suit. This was a purely practical decision as I did not want to have to rush out of my tent in the middle of the night with a bad case of explosive diarrhoea and have to worry about getting out of an all in one suit – it may not have lasted too long if I was not quick enough.

As well as the Tyvek suit I also took a pair of long Skins compression tights and a merino wool jumper. The latter is said to wick naturally and to resist the build up of odours. It does what it says on the tin. Despite using it all day on the second stage, during the overnight phase of the long stage and sleeping in it most nights it did not pong at any time.

My intention was to take the Tyvek suit as well as the Skins and merino wool top with me to the base camp and after an overnight stay to decide which to take with me and which to send back with the rest of my luggage to Ouarzazete. Because of the weather we faced and the need to be evacuated from the base camp, I did not have a chance to assess which to take. As a result I took both combinations, and was glad that I did as they were both needed, at times together, as it was very cold on some nights.

Although not strictly an item of clothing it was obvious that I would need sunglasses and that I also needed to give consideration to goggles in case of sand storms. For me the decision was complicated by virtue of the fact that I use contact lenses. My distance vision is reasonable, but not brilliant without my lenses, but with my lenses in place I find that I need glasses for reading.

I was very concerned at the thought of putting lenses in and out of my eyes in less than ideal hygiene conditions. In addition I did not want the additional weight which I would have had if I had used my normal monthly lenses and had to take cleaning fluids with me. Two options relating to lenses were available – either to use long-term lenses, and leave them in all the time, or go for daily disposable lenses. My optometrist was very unhappy about the idea of using long term lenses in the circumstances that I would be facing. I accepted her advice. I certainly did not want to have to pull out of the event because of an eye infection or ulceration, or more importantly risk permanent damage to my eyes. I remained concerned about the hygiene issues relating even to daily disposable lenses.

I found the perfect answer for me with Adidas Evil Eye professional sunglasses. These glasses provided me with a traditional sunglass. They also allowed me to have an optical insert made to my own eye prescription which clipped inside the sunglasses. The tinted lens could be replaced by a clear lens for the overnight phase of the long stage or around camp. In addition the hinges could be quickly removed and replaced by a head band and I felt that this combined with a buff pulled up over my face would be adequate if I faced a sand storm. The final advantage was that I could simply slip the glasses off if I needed to read the road map at any stage without having to take a pair of reading spectacles with me. Another box was ticked.

CHAPTER TEN

FOOD, COOKING AND SALT TABLETS

Rule 24 includes information about food, stipulating that each competitor must have a minimum of 14,000 calories, in other words, 2,000 calories per day. This seems a woefully inadequate amount of food to be consumed while tackling such an event, although I understand that some competitors in order to travel light keep to this minimal amount.

Two thousand calories is the amount I need to stay alive without weight loss when not taking any exercise. During the peak of my training I was consuming vast amounts of food and hardly ever stopped eating.

My normal daily intake was to start the day with a large breakfast and during the morning I would then eat two pieces of fruit and scoff away at nuts and dried fruit. Lunchtime was a large helping of pasta and then during the afternoon I would repeat the fruit and nuts. As soon as I arrived home I would make a sandwich to keep me going until my evening meal, which was followed by cheese and biscuits. More often than not I would be raiding the fridge for a final snack before I went to bed.

How on earth was I going to survive on 2,000 calories? The simple answer is that this was not an option for me. I did, however, need to compromise as the more calories I carried the heavier the weight of my kit, resulting in greater energy expenditure and longer out in the heat on the trails and dunes. In practice I ended up with between 2,500 and 3,200 calories each day. The higher figure was for the long stage, as I would need food for overnight. At the last minute I was seriously concerned that I did not have enough and so I threw in a bag containing three deserts with a total of a further 2000 calories. It was important that during the event I did not start to raid the next day's supplies if I was hungry and this extra supply was intended in case I needed to top up on my calories at any time. In practice the amount of food I took with me was more than adequate and, despite not eating all that I took with me, I returned home weighing exactly the same as the day I left.

I needed to make sure that as well as having enough calories I also had food which was palatable enough to be eaten. I felt it was important to try the food out before I was eating it for real in the desert. I was surprised that some other competitors had not tried out their food beforehand and as a result although they had enough calories in theory, when it came to reality they found their food unpalatable and were leaving a lot uneaten. During the event some competitors had spare food and this was being passed around. Again I decided to stick to the food which I had with me and had tested in advance. I did not want to find out in the middle of the Sahara that I was not able to tolerate any food, gels or powders which I had not tried before and end up with a stomach upset.

I started to purchase and try some foods in February 2008. I was staying in the Lake District for my 30th Wedding Anniversary. It was an ideal opportunity to go into some of the camping shops and buy some of the many makes of dehydrated food available – Mountain House, Travellunch, Backpacker's Pantry. The weight for some of these was however fairly high for the number of calories available.

I eventually came across the Expedition food range, which provides one of the highest calorie intakes per weight. I enjoy my food normally and the hotter and spicier the better. I am also, however, fortunate in that I can tolerate most food even if it is not particularly appetising. One of the problems with trying to increase the number of calories while keeping the weight down is that this can only be achieved by increasing the proportion of fat and reducing carbohydrates and protein. I actually found most of the Expedition Food range to be reasonable to eat, although even for me beef and potato casserole was disgusting. I did not

10 – FOOD, COOKING AND SALT TABLETS

even try the chocolate chip mousse desert as the reports were enough to warn me away from it.

As well as taking the Expedition foods I also took some breakfasts which I had made up for myself. I decided I would not be able to tolerate porridge with options of either added sultanas or strawberries every morning. I made up a packet of Jordan's muesli to which I added skimmed milk. All I then needed was to add water and as well as providing an alternative breakfast this reduced the number of fuel tablets I needed to carry, as this was eaten cold whereas the porridge and other Expedition foods were rehydrated with hot water.

The other action I took was to repackage all the Expedition foods. These come in aluminium packets and the actual weight is significantly higher than the dried weight indicated on the packet. By putting the dried food into Poly-Lina bags I was able to reduce the weight of each packet by approximately 15g (approximately half an ounce). This does not sound a lot but with 14 packets in total this was a weight saving of 210g (nearly half a pound), a lot of weight when it has to be carried for 150 miles. The other advantage of repackaging the food was that it could be made more compact and this made it easier to get everything into the rucksack.

The food for each day was then wrapped in separate parcels with cling film in order to keep it compact and placed in a plastic freezer bag with the number of calories for each day listed in case of spot checks by the organisers.

In addition I took a few sweets with me as a treat! Surprisingly Peanut M&Ms survive the heat, as do Jelly Babies. The main advantage of having some sweets with me was on the last day when local children came out looking for "bon-bons". They appreciated what I had left and they acted as a useful bribe to allow me to get a photograph.

The dried food needed to be reconstituted by adding hot water. I heated this in a Tibetan Titanium 900 mug weighing 130g (0.28lb), using a Tibetan titanium tablet stove which weighed a mere 10g (less than half an ounce). The heat was provided from Hexamine tablets. These had to be ordered from the organisers and collected when we arrived as they are obviously strictly forbidden on flights either as hand luggage or in the hold. The fuel tablets were protected from the wind by an aluminium wind shield. I had purchased a lighter, but at the last minute was advised by a GP colleague, one of the rare ones who still smokes, that it was totally unreliable and at the last minute parted with yet more money to get a better version.

I had a spork (a single utensil doubling up as a spoon and a fork) and I dispensed with plates or bowls and reused the plastic bottles which had been given to us with water in. Cut down, the base made an ideal bowl for food and the top was good for a brew of tea, which I enjoyed when I first got back to camp at the end of the day. This brew was also accompanied by a chicken noodle snack or creamy cheese pasta. I knew that I would need to eat something shortly after finishing each day but did not want to have my main meal at about 4pm as I knew I would be famished by bedtime if I did.

I also had to make decisions about what to eat during the day while completing each stage. I opted for a variety of different food bars (Cliff Bars, Torq Bars, Mule Bars and Honey Stinger Energy Bars), one peperami each day, a mix of nuts, raisins and dried fruit along with one sports energy gel each day. The advantage of taking the bars was that if I did not use them during the day they would make a "desert" for later when back at camp. A number of people take gels and powders, the latter being dissolved in the water bottle. They provide a low number of calories for their weight, and when warm can be foul tasting. I therefore decided to take just one Honey Stinger gel for each day. I love the taste of honey and psychologically I felt it would help towards the end of the day when I needed a last push to get back to the bivouac to take a gel, which in my mind if not in reality, would provide a quick hit of energy.

The final consideration was salt and other mineral replacements. The organisers hand out salt tablets and are very insistent that they should be taken regularly. Each tablet contains 500mgs of salt. The instructions provided when they were handed out varied from no advice at all, to two tablets per bottle up to six tablets per bottle, and this appears to purely depend upon who hands them out. There is a lot of debate in

10 – FOOD, COOKING AND SALT TABLETS

scientific papers about how necessary they actually are. In practice I did take some on most days, but not in the quantities advised. I also had with me Nuun tablets, which provide a smaller amount of salt and in addition provide magnesium, potassium and other minerals. I used one in alternative 800 ml bottles which I was carrying. Again I am not convinced about the real benefit of these but at the very least they made the warm water tastier and therefore more pleasant to drink.

CHAPTER ELEVEN

LUXURY ITEMS AND PACKING

The really serious competitors strip their kit to an absolute minimum. They even go to the stage of removing toggles and spare strapping off their rucksacks. I wanted to keep my kit weight down as much as possible but as I was there to complete and not compete I was happy to have a few "luxury items" with me.

In the event I opted for only two.

Firstly, I took a camera. It is unlikely that I will ever visit the Sahara again. I had already before setting off been asked to do talks to various organisations on my return and these would need to be illustrated. I also enjoy photography. I would have loved to have taken my digital SLR and a variety of lenses with me but this was never going to be an option. Instead I treated myself to a new compact camera. After considerable research I went for the Panasonic Lumix DMC-TZ5. I could have gone for a lighter and more compact camera but this particular model appeared to suit all of my requirements and in particular had a very impressive (for a compact camera) 10 x zoom. I felt this would be very useful. A spare battery and a spare memory card completed this first luxury item.

All of my training had been completed with a Garmin 305 GPS watch and a heart rate monitor. I wanted to take this with me. It would allow me to keep an eye on my heart rate, would record the distance I had travelled and allow me on return to plot the course that I had run, the distance I had ascended and a variety of other statistics, which appeals to my mathematical mind. The only problem is that the battery on the watch only lasts for about 10 hours and so in addition I had to take with me a solar charger (I used a Solio). I had tried out this combination before and found that it worked well and that the charge from the watch coupled with the charge from the solar charger allowed the watch to run for over 30 hours. I am not sure why but this did not work out in practice and the watch failed after about 14 hours on the long stage. In addition and to my frustration my heart rate monitor did not work at all, even though it had worked during all my training and right up to the last training session.

In order to keep the weight down I dismantled the charging unit for the watch and took out a metal plate which serves no real purpose and saved myself 25g (just under one ounce). It all adds up!

There were other luxury items which I could have taken but decided against. The main one, which was a possibility, was my iPod. I normally don't listen to music when I am out training, even when doing very long training sessions and so although I realised it may be of value overnight on the long stage I decided to leave it behind. I also wanted to experience the event and felt that listening to music could distract me from the sights, smells and sounds of the Sahara. I did not miss it.

The one item which I had not thought about and which might have been a good idea was a pillow. A number of people had an inflatable pillow and I am sure that was a better option than the stony ground or using my rucksack. I can't think of everything.

Underwear, a towel, a book or other luxuries were never an option. One of the members of my tent did however have a book with him and tore out the pages as he read them. They then served an additional useful purpose!

I now had everything I needed and instead of being scattered around the house, in bedrooms, lounge and hallway they were assembled all together in one place. My rucksack was placed alongside. There was no possible way that all of those items could get inside one small rucksack. At least that was my initial thought.

Ideally, for ease of access, it would have been good to have packed all my food at the bottom of the rucksack and my sleeping bag and thermarest towards the top. However, it is sensible to pack a rucksack with the heavier items towards the top as this is better from the point of not affecting my centre of gravity. I had watched a programme on ITV 4 about the Marathon des Sables a few months earlier and one of the lessons that I had learnt was that I needed to have my bag planned and organised and know where everything was. Some competitors the previous year appeared to have planned the packing of their rucksacks using chaos theories as the underlying principle.

I set to and somehow one item after another gradually disappeared inside my rucksack. The food was placed at the top and with some careful manoeuvring of the zips everything was inside and the job was done. I had also reached my other target and my rucksack was approximately 10kgs (22lbs).

My planning and preparation, as well as my physical training were now complete. I was as ready as possible to start the 24th Marathon des Sables.

(The full kit list including food is shown in Appendix 1.)

PART FOUR

THE BIVOUAC,
THE ORGANISATION
AND TENT 95

CHAPTER TWELVE

THE BIVOUAC, THE ORGANISATION AND TENT 95

"Y'allah! Y'allah!" is the cry that greeted us each morning at about 6am as we were emerging from our sleeping bags into the cold at the beginning of the day. The berbers were about to remove our tent. It made no difference if you were still in your sleeping bag, cooking food or doing anything else to prepare for the day ahead. Three or four berbers arrived at the tent and without ceremony and in a matter of a few seconds the tent was collapsed backwards and lay on the floor waiting to be folded up and taken away. A short while later, the blankets on the floor of the tent were also removed and everyone was left in the open to finish off their preparations for the day ahead.

Approximately 100 tents and the blankets were then loaded on to lorries to be transported to the next bivouac and reassembled, ready for when we arrived at the end of the next stage. In addition all the tents – and in their cases proper tents with guy ropes and a front and back and not just sides – for the organisers, medics, photographers and press had to be dismantled and transported.

It is only when you actually see all this happening around you that it is possible to begin to grasp the sheer size of the task that the organisers face in putting on this event in the desert.

With over 800 competitors and more than 400 organisers, press etc.

this is a small village on the march for nine days in a hostile environment. As well as the main organisers there are course markers, marshals, time keepers, water distributors, doctors, nurses and physiotherapists, technical staff, press and photographers.

As well as the tents for competitors and organisers there are tents for email facilities, a tent for faxing and phone calls, tents for the medical team and on the first and last days when food is provided "restaurant" tents to feed over 1200 people.

The bivouac is organised with the competitor's tents arranged together, with tents allocated according to the country of the competitors. All the UK entrants were therefore in the same area of the camp site.

Each tent houses eight people and it is necessary for everyone to organise themselves into a group of eight, and then find a tent. This normally occurs at the base camp on the first night, on a first come first served basis. As the base camp was evacuated this year because of the weather we were not able to get into tents until the end of the first stage. Some people had not formed up into groups at this stage and were wandering around the camp looking for a tent which did not have its full complement. This must have been an additional difficulty at the end of a long day, but fortunately not one which I faced as eight of us had already organised ourselves together.

The first member of the tent whom I met was Russell Muldoon. Russell had been having difficulty getting an ECG and medical certificate completed by his doctor. He had noticed that I was one of the entrants and that I was a doctor who was within 50 miles of where he lived. He contacted me and I arranged to meet up with him about two weeks before the event. He arrived at my surgery on a Friday night just after 6pm after a long journey from London, where he had been working that day.

We chatted for a while and I examined him and then commenced to do his ECG. To my horror the report automatically generated by the machine stated that he had an abnormal ECG. This would not normally bother me. Firstly the machine often over reports, suggesting there are problems where none exist. Secondly as a well trained athlete, as everyone needs to be for this event, it is very common for apparent abnormalities to be present. (Like any muscle the heart muscle increases in size with exercise).

I would normally have been happy to accept his ECG and sign him off as being fit. I did not know at that stage how strict the medical scrutiny would be on the admin day before we started running. I was concerned that if I removed the computer generated report they might be suspicious and if I stated that the abnormalities were not significant, that they may not agree. I did not want to be standing next to Russell the day before the event was due to start and find he was thrown out on the basis of an ECG which I had passed as being normal.

Fortunately I managed to arrange for him to see a local cardiologist who was available the next day. He had an Echocardiogram, which not surprisingly was normal and I signed off his ECG and medical certificate. As it happened his ECG was hardly looked at on the check day and there had been no need for any concern.

I discovered that Russell was not the most organised member of the tent! Admittedly he had been very busy with his work before we set off but there were a few items of kit missing (spare batteries for his head torch for example) and while in the tent if anything was misplaced it was likely to be something that belonged to Russell.

During the event he unfortunately had problems with his feet and gaiters, as well as being unwell and on the overnight phase of the long stage temporarily got lost. Despite all the problems he kept going, although I am sure there were times when he felt like packing in. Every respect and well done to Russell for a great achievement.

During my training I had four sessions in the heat chamber at John Moore's University in Liverpool. On the morning of my last session Ben Edwards (Senior Lecturer in Chronobiology and Environmental Physiology) who had arranged the sessions and had himself completed the Marathon des Sables a few years earlier arranged for myself and two of the others who had been using the heat chamber to meet up. Another two "Scouse" entrants were able to join us.

As a result I was able to meet Joe Skinner, Richard Webster, Rob Jackson and Jonathan Kane. Joe, Richard and Rob were part of Tent 95.

Jonathan had already made arrangements to join other people he knew in a different tent, but it was good to have met someone else and to keep meeting him around the camp. His feet got absolutely trashed on the long stage and I have complete respect for his ability to continue and do the final marathon stage, and in a very respectable time.

Joe is a solicitor on the Wirral – although this would have been difficult to believe if you had seen him after he had had a Number 1 haircut in Erfoud before we set off into the desert. It would have been a problem to differentiate him from his less welcome clients.

Joe's background is as a rugby player. He played at a younger age as a professional in France until his career was cut short by a rugby injury. He is built more like the hooker that he used to be than an elite marathon and ultra marathon runner. Despite that and problems with blisters and sickness and a very painful foot which meant he was still hobbling slowly and painfully as we travelled back to Gatwick, Joe completed the whole event. Joe showed a huge degree of toughness and like every member of our tent I hold his achievement in complete respect.

Richard was the runner in our tent. Whereas the rest of us were interested in completing the event Richard was there to compete and get a good time and position. He has a marathon time of under 3 hours 15 minutes and this means that for his age (43 years) he has an automatic entry to the London Marathon, which he was planning to run three weeks after our return [and completed in a time of 2 hours 53 minutes and 9 seconds].

Richard had a great race, improving on his finishing position every day and ending up in 135th position overall. Although he was obviously very pleased, and rightly so, I know that he feels he could improve on this based on what he learned during the event.

Richard was the member of the tent who kept an eye out for everyone else and was always there to give a helping hand, boiling water, sorting out food and generally offering any help he could. It was a privilege to meet such a nice guy and an excellent athlete who can be very proud of what he achieved.

Rob, the last member of our tent whom I met while still in the UK,

12 – THE BIVOUAC, THE ORGANISATION AND TENT 95

is a Nurse Clinician in Liverpool. He is not basically a runner and only really started to run because he wanted to do the Marathon des Sables. He had obviously got himself very fit, although this did not particularly show in the first few days. However, he had a great day on the marathon stage and showed a great deal of determination and ability. He again continued and finished despite blisters and illness.

Rob has a great singing voice. At least I believe he has but the tent was never entertained by him. Another reason for meeting up in the future now that we have all completed the 24th Marathon des Sables. I think he had the best sense of humour in the tent – that of a typical scouser.

I know on his return he was looking forward to getting back to a game of 5 a side football and to having a full English breakfast. Another great tent mate who did exceptionally well despite the problems he experienced.

I met the other three members of our tent at Gatwick airport and then finally in the hotel at Ouarzazete. Martin, Ant and Nick had met several of the others at either The Brecon Beacons race or the Grantham Canal race, which had been used as training events in readiness for the Marathon des Sables. They were the non scouser members of our tent, as the rest of us were all originally from the Liverpool area (or in some cases pseudo scousers from the Wirral).

Martin Hallworth, an engineer from Warrington, was at 53 the second oldest member of the tent, after me. He had met Richard while doing the Brecon Beacons and it was clear to me that although he may not be the fastest runner he was very determined and had the ability to just keep going and grind out the miles.

Martin was probably the quietest member of Tent 95 but he was also the intellectual member of the tent; at least if his ability in "Who wants to be a millionaire?" was anything to go by.

I thought Martin's race was over before it had even started. He managed to pull a calf muscle while jogging up a small sand dune the day before we started to run. I was convinced he would be unable to start or if he did that he would be unable to complete. I also wrote him off after the long stage when with a bout of diarrhoea and vomiting he looked absolutely like death. He was obviously struggling to get fluids or food inside him. He proved me wrong with his calf muscle injury and he proved me wrong with his stomach and bowel problems. A true star who was never going to give up and again demanding complete respect from me and everyone else in our tent.

The final two members of Tent 95, who had met Richard at Grantham Canal Race, were two brothers Ant Riley and Nick Zambelis. Ant and Nick are both originally from Zimbabwe but now live in the UK in Hatfield and Warwick respectively.

Ant is an engineer in full time employment and his wife works in London. During the day Ant has to do a demanding job, and then look after his four year old son when he gets home. He often was not able to start his training sessions until 8pm when his wife returned home from work in the City.

Ant carried with him the very distinctive flag of Zimbabwe and as a result was interviewed on a number of occasions by the press. He was also the member of our tent with the heaviest rucksack. Included in his kit were two magazines from which he read bedtime stories to the rest of the tent. They were not as uplifting as the Churchillian quotes which we heard being read out by a member of Tent 94 on the morning of the long stage in order to motivate his colleagues. They were however certainly more interesting and amusing.

Each competitor is issued at the start of the event with a medical card which has to be hole punched whenever medical assistance is sought. One section is for pain killers, one for anti-inflammatory drugs and one for other treatments. I managed to keep my card intact while Richard had just one hole punched in his. By comparison Ant had a card which looked as if someone had taken a pot shot at it with a shot gun.

I think Ant was secretly a little disappointed with his time and position. I cannot begin to imagine how difficult it must have been to train with the added responsibilities of a full time job and his young child. To then take part and finish despite the blisters and other foot problems and the sickness and diarrhoea that he experienced means he can be hugely proud, as were the rest of the tent, of what he achieved.

Nick, at 27, was the youngest member of the tent. His main sporting interests are cricket and hockey. He bought a stick in Erfoud and organised a game of cricket in the Hotel Kasbah where we had the administration day. Perhaps it was not a good idea for one of the team to hit one of the doctors very firmly in the leg with the tennis ball we were using, particularly as Nick required treatment from the same medic a few days later.

It was Nick with a random comment on the first night during a lull in the conversation who provided Tent 95 with its motivation for the whole event and a unifying theme which kept us together and focussed for the whole week. In order to avoid any legal repercussions further details will not be revealed and the secret will remain with the members of Tent 95.

Nick on one occasion told me that he was not particularly good at commitment. I don't think he was referring to his commitment to the Marathon des Sables and to completing the event. In the same way that I wrote Martin off, I was also certain having passed Nick vomiting at the side of the track on Stage 2 that his race was over. His complete commitment proved me wrong. Despite all the problems he experienced Nick finished in third position in the tent and again I totally respect his achievement.

Tent 95 was a united tent from the day we all first met. Eight strangers thrown together in stressful and physically demanding circumstances could have been a recipe for disaster, arguments and disagreements. At no stage was there any problem between any of those of us in the tent and strong and permanent friendships have been forged. Every member of Tent 95 had complete respect for what every other member achieved.

The full results of the entire tent are shown in Appendix 2.

PART FIVE

MY DIARY

CHAPTER THIRTEEN

OFF TO MOROCCO AND THE SAHARA DESERT STORMS

25TH MARCH 2009 – D MINUS 4

After all the planning, training and organising I eventually set off today to head to Morocco for the 24th Marathon des Sables – "the toughest footrace on earth".

Following a very pleasant lunch with Cherith (seafood pasta at the River Wyre) I got to Poulton-le-Fylde station at about 2pm. Said our goodbyes – I am sure much harder for Cherith than for me as I am heading off to do something I want to do, to face new experiences and take on the biggest challenge of my life. Cherith is left behind to carry on as normal, although without me around, and I know she will be very concerned about me and hoping that I will be alright.

I had an excellent journey – arrived at Euston at 5.15 (about 5 minutes late) and then straight onto underground to Victoria for Gatwick Express, arriving at Gatwick at about 6.15.

I had booked into Sofitel Hotel near North Terminal. I had decided that I would spoil myself rather than stay in a Travel Lodge or similar which some others are using – won't be many luxuries next week. A very impressive hotel – and when I booked in at reception I was advised that due to room availability I was being upgraded to a luxury room. It was as if they knew that I was going to be roughing it next week.

I had a choice of three restaurants so I decided to stay in the hotel to eat. I had an excellent meal of sea bream fillet with Mediterranean vegetables and new potatoes, helped down with a very acceptable glass of red wine. This was followed up with cheese and biscuits and a coffee before turning in for an early night. I kept falling asleep while watching the news.

My cold which has been present all week appears to be a little better and hopefully will continue to improve before Sunday.

26TH MARCH 2009 – D MINUS 3

Today has seen us arrive in Morocco. I started the day with a good full English breakfast – have to enjoy these meals as next week will consist of dehydrated foods, muesli and energy bars!

Arriving at the airport at about 10am was interesting as the queue for checking in consisted of 200 plus entrants for the Marathon des Sables and most of us had the same distinctive red Raidlight rucksacks.

I met up with Russell and then met Jo, Richard and Rob who I met last week in Liverpool and also Martin – so that is six of us for our eight man tent.

An uneventful flight to Ouarzazete, although we were afforded some good views of the snow covered Atlas Mountains. It is probably my ignorance but am not quite sure why this town exists or why it has an airport. Ours was the only plane in sight and after it had unloaded and refuelled it departed with just the pilot and flight crew on board.

Despite being the only plane to arrive it took us over an hour to get through passport control and then another queue at the hotel to get room keys – so despite it being only a five minute transfer time from the airport it was two hours after we landed before we got to our room.

I am sharing a room with Russell. We have a good spacious room – one bedroom each with a small sitting area, a toilet and a bathroom. Dropped our luggage and headed straight to the nearest shop to stock up

Training on the sand dunes near Blackpool

Ice on beach

Training in the Lakes - Elterwater

"Good Hope" – I hoped this was not to be an omen

My kit ready to be packed

My packed rucksack with trekking poles and water bottles

The view from coach window heading to the Sahara

The first base camp - a mud bath

Digging trenches to drain water away from tent

Base camp shortly before evacuating

Hail stones in Erfoud, on the edge of the Sahara

At last we reached the starting line

Trying not to show my nerves before the start

Time to rest and take a few photographs

A typical dunes view

Abandoned village - with satellite dish

Approaching a check-point

Spectacular views

Competitor's tents

Competitor's tents at dusk

Tent 95 (from Left) Nick, Ant, Rob, Richard, Joe, Martin, Russell and Steve

Time for some much needed rest

Steve in Dunes

Compass bearings on route sign

The longest run in ever!

Paris Opera concert in the Sahara

The final sand dunes

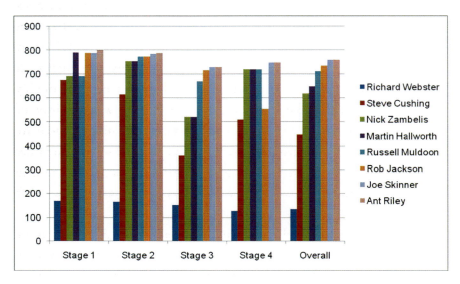

Tent 95 finishing positions for each stage and overall

on water – over £5 for 6 x 1.5 litre bottles. But essential whatever the price. Joined the other members of our tent for a beer and some food – avoided the chicken and fresh fruit, apart from an orange which I could peel. Also met up with Ant and Nick – two brothers, initially from Zimbabwe and now living in Hatfield and Warwick – who make our tent complement of eight. It is already very clear that we are going to have an amusing week – had a good laugh so far and only likely to get better.

I turned in at ten – last chance to sleep in a bed for another eight nights..

27TH MARCH 2009 – D MINUS 2

It is almost impossible to put into words the experiences of the last 24 hours. If there is a sense of frustration as you read this, then if you read on you will understand where it comes from.

The coach was due to leave the hotel at nine yesterday morning. Russell and I arrived at the coach at just after 8.30am to be told that the coaches had been rescheduled for 8am – we had not received the telephone call! The coaches eventually left at 9am for what was meant to be a six hour journey. We had only just set off when the rain started. To call it rain is an understatement and does not do it justice. For the whole journey there was a torrential downpour. Dried out river beds were in full flow. It was almost impossible to see out of the window, which was probably useful. Our coach driver considered himself to be the Lewis Hamilton of the coach driving world. He obviously thought it was compulsory to drive in the boot of the car in front, and believed that single solid white lines down the centre of the road were an indication to overtake. He also thought his coach had a 4 wheel drive facility as he kept trying a bit of off road driving.

Eventually at about 4pm we came to a halt. We had had to travel a different route to that planned as one of the road bridges was not passable due to the amount of rain that had fallen. (The French and German competitors had flown into Ouarzazate in the morning and left a couple of hours after us and were not able to get more than a short distance before the roads became impassable due to the amount of rain.) At about 4.15pm we transferred to a lorry for a very bumpy 25 minutes to the camp, with a lorry driver who also had been watching too much of Lewis Hamilton. Even when we arrived the site was already a quagmire. Russell and I were the first from our tent of eight to arrive so we struggled across the mud field to get a tent. The tents are made of hessian with sides but no front or back, and a tarpaulin cover. The rain was dripping through the hessian and onto the sleeping area and we were digging channels in the ground to try to divert the water.

I had put sun cream on before we left the hotel. Grease or whatever it is cross channel swimmers use would have been better as we were shivering with cold. I put on two pullovers and the jacket and jeans I had travelled in from the UK and got a bin-bag liner to keep some rain off. When we heard that the French and Germans would not make it we pinched their tarpaulins to make a front to our tent. By this time we had been joined by Ant and Nick.

At about 7pm we headed across to the organisers area for some food. I put flip flops on as the mud would have ruined any shoes. Within a few yards my flip flops had been sucked off my feet and disappeared into two or three inches of mud, to be rescued by hand, as I could not actually see them. Eventually gave up and for much of the time I went bare footed. By this time the ground made Glastonbury on a bad day look like a picnic during a drought.

As we reached the organisers tents we were informed that the camp was being evacuated and that we were going back by lorry to a hotel. Several of the other coaches had been held back in the nearest town and were also heading to the hotel without going out to the camp at all.

We had to head back to our tent and get our luggage and then back to the organisers' tents before eating. By this time the first group had gone back by lorry and we had to wait an hour for the lorries to return. As we eventually arrived back at the nearest town at about 10pm we crossed a bridge and the water was flowing rapidly and almost up to the bridge; that is until we got half way across and found the water was actually flowing over the bridge. We got into the hotel and were allocated our room – with one double bed – and I only met Russell two weeks ago to do his ECG as a favour – hope I don't get struck off!

28ᵀᴴ MARCH 2009 – D MINUS 1

Apparently at about 4 this morning there was a further downpour with thunder and lightning. Headed down to breakfast at just after 7am and eventually at about 8.30am the announcement we had been dreading, but expecting, was made. Day 1 has been cancelled. So no matter what happens I cannot say I have ever really done the Marathon des Sables. We are staying at the hotel tonight and further information will be provided later today. At present they are not able to dismantle the camp site, as the tents are too wet, and as it has rained most of the morning they have had no chance to start to dry.

We are trying to have a good laugh but everyone is thoroughly pissed off and feeling totally frustrated. The unspoken fear is that the next announcement will be the cancellation of Day 2. To be absolutely honest I am not entirely sure at present that the event will take place. The ground is now mud and the dried out river beds we were meant to run on will now be full flowing rivers. The sheer logistics of getting the show on the road may prove too much.

I first thought about entering this event 20 years ago. I wrote my first cheque on 20th April 2006, and for the last 12 months it has dominated my life, with hours of training and planning and a large expense. The thought that it may not happen is difficult to take on board. In addition it will impact on my fundraising for those kids in Watamu who so desperately need support. Psychologically it will prove difficult to prepare myself again even if we do get informed that we are starting albeit on a reduced course. That is why I am frustrated, and as I sit in an internet cafe in a town whose name I don't even know it is difficult to fight back a few justifiable tears.

I can only hope and wait and see what transpires over the next 24 hours.

I left the internet café having written the above which I sent as an email and on my way back got soaked again by a further downpour of rain, with claps of thunder all around. I had lunch and as we came out the sun also came out and we saw the first blue sky since we arrived. Everyone started to sit around the pool as it was quite warm. After a while I decided to go for a walk as I could not stand all the rumours that were being passed around causing anxiety but with no accurate information.

I wandered towards the market which we had visited earlier in the morning – a real challenge to my sense of smell. I met up with Joe and we headed to one of the stalls where it was possible to buy sheets of plastic. We bought eight one meter lengths – one for each of us in the tent. Who would have thought I would have been heading to the Marathon des Sables and buying ground sheets for our tent to keep us dry!

We were also joined by Russell and on the way back, having had a quick look at one of the local shops, we stopped at the barbers as Joe decided he wanted a number 1 haircut. From there it was directly into a bar – purely to escape the weather again – this time a deluge of hailstones.

By the time we got back to the hotel the announcement had already been made – race on! What a sense of relief – and now time to get my head back into gear ready to start Stage 2 on Monday.

One of the press photographers has told us that the press has been told that that the race will be 242 kilometres (just over 150 miles). If that is the case then my fears that this will not be a true Marathon des Sables have been replaced by a realisation that this could be one of the hardest. The road book, which we had been given as we travelled by coach through the deluge, had indicated a longer than normal event at 252 kilometres (just over 156 miles). If it really is 242K then they have only cut 10 kilometres (6 miles) in total and as the first day was meant to be 30 kilometres (18.5 miles) they will have to extend the other days by a total of 20 kilometres (12 miles) and the whole distance – which is longer than some previous events – will have to be run over 5/6 days and not 6/7 days. In addition the dried out river beds are likely to be very muddy, although in parts there may be a superficial dried out top surface with mud immediately beneath and good for the shoes to sink into.

The "notice board" in the hotel has a list on it of items needed by other runners – unbelievable but it includes:

- Compass
- Signalling mirror
- Power and energy drinks
- Insoles size 8 to 9.

It also includes some humorous items like one tent seeking a housekeeper, etc.

29TH MARCH 2009 – "D DAY"

Should have started running today! Instead we have to go to another hotel for the planned administration checks which should have happened yesterday in the desert.

I set my alarm for 7am and got up to organise my bags and kit. I put my watch on and noticed it was 6.24am! I had set my alarm on my phone and hadn't taken account of the fact that my phone automatically adjusts for British Summer Time – which hasn't caught on in Morocco. I was not the only one to have done this and lots of us were milling around waiting for breakfast to start.

We had to finalise our bags in order to leave hotel at 8.30am for the admin check. Final decisions as anything I still have with me and not in my luggage returning to Ouarzazete will have to be carried nearly 150 miles. But more importantly anything not in my rucksack is not coming with me – even if I need it.

Fortunately we were right at the front of the queue when we arrived at the Hotel Kasbah and I was probably 20th in for checking. All done in ten minutes:

- Show ID

- Collect number
- Electronic tag for timing attached to bag
- Kit check, i.e.
  - completed form handed in with signed declaration
  - asked weight of bag
  - asked weight of food (no visual check or weighing)
- Issued distress flare and salt tablets (no instructions)
- Medical certificate looked at
- ECG "checked" (looked at by running a finger along each lead print out with most scrutiny given to was lead V2 – due to electrical interference!)
- Pick up pre-ordered fuel tablets
- Finished.

I thought we were then heading back to our hotel but have to stay at hotel where admin check is taking place while everyone else is processed until about 4pm – six hours hanging around. Sunny day so after an hour or so went for a wander across the road (Richard, Rob, Joe, Martin, Russell and myself) and had a walk and a gentle jog on the small sand dunes. Martin ran a few yards – and then came to a grinding halt; has pulled a calf muscle. He is now hobbling around using a trekking pole – I think he will seriously struggle tomorrow.

I think my bag weighs about 10.5kgs (23lbs) – the lightest probably in the tent. Nick had his bag weighed at about 16kgs (just over 35lbs) and Ant is a frightening weight at almost 18kgs (almost 40lbs) – before water. I think that he will find that a real problem.

Had lunch and just sitting in bar writing up diary. One of the Ahansal brothers- the likely winner – is sitting opposite us. His bag weighs 7.5kgs (16.5lbs) – 5kgs (11lbs) is food.

Another two hours to fill before briefing and then back to the hotel. Would like to get back early as I want to get to pharmacy – my cold is not as bad but think I am developing cold sore and would like some Zovirax. Six days without a shave would make me look bad enough without a whopping cold sore on my upper lip.

Eventually at about 4.15pm the official announcements are made. The main reason for delay is that this is a media event – not a good reason to keep 800 athletes hanging around for up to seven hours the day before such an event.

Although there was an English translation it was still difficult to understand what is happening. It would appear following discussions with other people that the hope of a 242 k Marathon des Sables can be forgotten. At the moment an altered day 2 and day 3 appear to be happening but no guarantees after that.

We will be picked up at our hotel at 7am tomorrow and taken to where Day 2 should have started and where Day 1 started last year. That means that after 1.7 K – just over 1 mile – we will be into sand hills and tough ones at that. However, we will not be following the road map and the original route. We will be running a loop and that means of course that we will be sleeping where we should have been sleeping at the end of today's run. No idea at present where or how far we will go on Tuesday; or what, if anything, will happen after that. [It eventually transpired that I had misunderstood the information and that the first day was a run to a new base camp and that the following day was the loop day returning to the same camp for a further night.]

I think it leaves more questions than answers and what wasn't said is more significant than what was said.

It may be that we are running a loop tomorrow because the route from the end of the first stretch of dunes at about 14 kilometres (8.7 miles) to a new base camp is not passable. It may also be that there is concern about safety and / or weather and they want to finish at a point where they can evacuate again if necessary.

Day 3 is a total uncertainty.

It may be that no commitment to Days 4 to 7 is because they don't want to commit publicly and then have to change plans and cancel the rest of event. They are obviously seriously concerned about the potential damage to the Marathon des Sables brand name if they don't complete the event but also if they continue and there are risks and as a result serious problems arise. None of us are equipped for this weather after all.

I have also been told – maybe another of the many rumours – that thunderstorms are predicted for mid-week. They may be hedging their bets to see what happens.

Whatever we will probably be running tomorrow. Need to try to get my head around the idea, summon up some enthusiasm and enjoy the day taking in as much of the atmosphere and scenery as possible.

At the end of the media event / announcements we had to get coaches back to hotel. No information as to the process and not enough coaches for all to go in one journey. Tried to get out of the hotel but they were funnelling everyone through a tiny gap. I think they were trying to check the electronic timing tags. Eventually they appeared to give up and everyone was let through in one fell swoop – but the coaches were full so I had to stand in cold and windy conditions and shivering for over forty minutes until the coaches returned.

I eventually got back to the hotel and had a run (to warm up) to pharmacy to get some Zovirax and to internet café to send an email. The meal tonight was not very good. I had a beer and then time for bed at 10pm as due to get up at 6am tomorrow.

It is not looking good for Martin. Everyone else is obviously frustrated but at least we can make some sort of start tomorrow. I cannot imagine how he must be feeling at this stage.

CHAPTER FOURTEEN

STAGE 1
ERG CHERBI TO ERG ZNAIGUI
19.5 MILES

30ᵀᴴ MARCH 2009

What a fantastic day. After all the stress and frustration of the last few days the 24th Marathon des Sables finally got under way. I was down for breakfast at 6am – well actually to get some hot water to make up an Expedition porridge with sultanas – I wanted to have my planned food rather than a hotel breakfast. It took about 20 minutes to sort everything out – day food into front pack on rucksack, Garmin watch on, P20 applied, bag repacked... I couldn't understand what had happened to Russell who eventually got back to room at five to seven as he thought we were leaving at 7.30! It was all a bit of a rush and I had to help him sort everything out before heading down to the hotel foyer to wait for the coaches. Our plan today for the tent is to be last away from the hotel, as we don't want to be hanging around at the start. All the coaches had left and we were still waiting, along with twelve other competitors, when four taxis turned up – five of us to a taxi plus the driver!

Our driver was Lewis Hamilton of the taxi world this time. There was a convoy in front of us of over twenty coaches and numerous 4x4 vehicles of the organisers. Our driver set off to overtake them all – until eventually behind the first lead vehicle. We then realised why he had been driving so fast when he pulled into a garage – apparently his fuel gauge was hard on empty, and he obviously wanted to top up but still be in touch with the rest of the convoy. He kept his engine running while filling up and at the same time carried on a conversation with the garage owner who stood smoking his cigarette just a few feet from the petrol pump – whatever happened to Moroccan health and safety regulations? Having filled up he then kept to the back of queue until we arrived.

I have never felt more apprehensive as we got closer and closer. It was amazing to actually see the traditional inflatables positioned at the start of the event. We all had to queue for our water supplies for the day and then yet another wait for final instructions. The temperature was 18.5 degrees C and the wind speed 3m/sec (another competitor with his "toys for boys" had a measuring instrument for temperature and wind speed). It actually felt really cold but I did not want to put extra layers on as I also knew they would soon have to come off once we started.

Almost on the dot of ten we were off. I decided to set off with Martin who amazingly has made it to the start line. The others set off jogging. It was initially very flat as we headed out to the dunes but we were only going at about 3 miles per hour so we were very close to the back – probably no more than 30 or 40 behind us. We caught up with Joe and Rob at about four miles and the four of us then went along at roughly the same pace for a while, but constantly stopping to take photographs.

The dunes were spectacular – they were massive with interesting shapes, contours and tones and an amazing smell of lavender. Probably not many will see the dunes with so much vegetation – a benefit of the weather of the last few days. I had been warned that the dunes would be frightening. They were tough but very doable and at no stage did I feel that I would not be able to cope.

Check-point 1 came up at 8.5 miles – having taken about three hours, during which time I had drunk 2.5 litres of water. My tactic is to spend as little time as possible at check points. I took my 3 litres of water and refilled my bottles and set off leaving Martin behind, with Joe and Rob somewhere further behind.

The section to check-point 2 was very flat and stony. The trail was very similar to what I experience in Tenerife. I managed to get my foot down and move at about 4 miles per hour to the next check-point. Just before reaching it I walked through a totally ruined village including its own derelict mosque. [It was only on returning and looking at my photographs that I also noticed the satellite dish!]

At check-point 2 – a total distance of 14 miles and a time of 4 hours and 30 minutes from the start – I followed the same tactics as at check-point 1 and as a result I went past Russell and Nick. (I did not realise until later that Ant had been left behind at check-point 1 as he was already in need of treatment for blisters). I continued at a similar pace until approximately three miles from the finish of the stage when I hit the final stretch of dunes. Again they were very beautiful but probably more difficult than the first stretch (as someone said they were "Beautiful from far; far from beautiful"). I still felt very good and so continued at a good pace and eventually topping the crest of the dunes could see the bivouac approximately one mile away in the distance. I eventually crossed the finishing line – 19.5 miles for the stage in 6 hours and 18 minutes and was 676th out of 812 starters.

Richard was first back from Tent 95 in 4 hours and 11 minutes, and had found a tent. However, it took me a while to find him and I had just settled in when Russell and Nick arrived. I got my feet elevated using a tent pole to rest them on to reduce any fluid which had accumulated during the day and lay there quietly while trying to get as much water in as possible. I checked my feet and was delighted to find I had no problems – just a small sore area on my left heel but no blisters.

After resting for about half an hour I boiled up my first lot of water for a welcome cup of tea and a creamy cheese pasta – acceptable without being brilliant.

The next job was to sort my bag out, as it is important to try to remain organised, not only for my own benefit but so as to not to intrude on the limited space for everyone else in the tent. Because of the small space in which to operate and the fact that my bag was tightly packed it was quite difficult and I kept putting things back in my bag and then finding I still needed them.

At about 7 o'clock I went to the email tent and eventually managed to get a message composed and sent. It was quite a task and I struggled with the French key board and also the fact that I had a limited number of words so had to recompose my message before it was ready to forward. When I got back to the tent, Martin, Rob, Joe and Ant were all back – not a bad way for Rob to celebrate his birthday.

My dinner tonight was spaghetti bolognese – it tasted good and I also had a fresh orange. Ant had carried it from Erfoud for Rob for his birthday – but he doesn't like them. I never turn food down, particularly a fresh piece of fruit.

As I write up my diary I am now lying in all my clothes and in my sleeping bag as it is getting very cold. The tent is having a game of "Who wants to be a millionaire?" with Nick as question master.

It is only 8.30pm but I think we may all be off to sleep soon. We have to get ready for apparently 22 plus miles tomorrow – I for one am looking forward to it!

CHAPTER FIFTEEN

STAGE 2
ERG ZNAIGUI TO ERG ZNAIGUI
22 MILES

31ST MARCH 2009

Today has been another good day after an awful night. First night in tent – and I am quite glad we missed one night now. The ground is so hard and the thermarest appears to make no difference. I think I must have exerted myself almost as much turning backwards and forwards and rolling from side to side trying to find a comfortable patch as I did on the run yesterday. My difficulty in sleeping wasn't helped by the snoring all around – no doubt I contributed as much as anyone. I was up three times for my normal pee, although I did not hold the tent record. I felt I hadn't slept but missed

- Nick throwing up
- Joe peeing times 6
- Rain.

Despite my apparent lack of sleep I felt OK when I woke up – just incredibly cold. After a short doze it was time to get out of my sleeping bag and start to sort myself out. I was moving packets of food in and out of my bag while trying to find my stove and fuel. Got that one sorted. Now what happened to the spork? Then time to get my rucksack packed up for the run and get my toe-toe socks on with some taping to my feet where I had noticed a few sores after yesterday's run. I was so cold that I put my Skins on my legs and my merino wool top on with my T shirt on top of that – needed to do it in that order as my race number is on my T shirt and it needs to be displayed at all times.

We all had to stand and wait for ten to fifteen minutes while Patrick Bauer did his announcements in French, with an English translation which was only partially understandable, with what could be understood being drowned out by the helicopter flying overhead. We were advised that the previous day the vast majority of us took a small detour on the course. Rather than the majority receiving a time penalty those who went the right way had fifteen minutes deducted from their times. It seemed an odd way of responding, but I suppose it was the same difference, and whichever way Rob was delighted as he had taken the right route.

As it was not quite the official starting time of 9 o'clock Patrick Bauer tried to get everyone to do some stretching exercises. Bizarre and the general feeling I am sure, like mine, was let's get off despite the time.

We set off on our way for the second day with 22 miles ahead of us and found we were heading straight into a strong headwind. It was fairly flat initially and then we were into undulating sand hills. There was lovely scenery off to the right of hills with beautiful lighting. As we approached check-point 1 at 8.25 miles there were some more minor sand hills. I took the opportunity to take my merino wool top off and apply sun cream but left my Skins on my legs. At the check-point I quickly filled up my water bottles and headed off along an almost flat trail. Or at least I did after I put the top back on my water bottle properly which I had not done initially and as a result the water was spilling out – fortunately I had picked up three litres of water at the check-point– but another lesson learned, as it could have been disastrous if I had had only one bottle of water and had lost most of it

The next section was a relatively boring run along a stony trail, with a hilly section over the last one to two miles until I eventually reached check-point 2 and with another 7.5 miles completed (not 6.8 miles as stated on the road map).

After continuing on a flat trail and feeling quite good I then hit the final two miles of sand hills. It was a bit like climbing a mountain where the top never appears and there is always another rise ahead – but this time another tough sand hill. The camp was visible but never seemed to get any nearer. However eventually after 22 miles covered in 6 hours and 40 minutes I reached the camp site. I was again pleased that my feet felt, and were OK, but it was good to be back at the tent.

Richard had already arrived back, in his all too familiar first position for Tent 95, but had left the tent for a wander so I had twenty minutes to myself to get my feet up on the tent pole and get some fluids in me. Once again I made a check of my feet, an essential and obsessive routine as a missed blister or sore no matter how minor could become a major problem. I had one sore area on my right heel and also one on my right great toe – neither was a major problem but will need taping tomorrow.

Richard returned and asked me how the others from the tent were getting on. I explained that I had been in front of Ant, Jo, Rob and Martin from the start but that Russell and Nick had set off jogging and had been ahead of me. I had caught up with them at 5.5 miles. Russell was having trouble with his feet but I thought he would be alright. However, Nick was being sick and looked ghastly. I was very dubious if he would make it back to the tent.

I tried to ease the discomfort from my shoulders and trapezius muscles which had developed from carrying my rucksack. I then brewed up and had a cup of tea followed by a chicken pasta before fiddling around with my bag – a frequent job. Suddenly walking into the tent were Martin and Nick – an amazing effort from both of them. Next in were Russell and Rob. Russell had had to stop to get his feet attended to by Doc Trotters – and had to revisit them on his arrival back at the tent. His feet are damned sore, so another amazing effort. Next in was Joe who is again struggling with his feet and Ant, just a short way behind, who as well as problems with his feet is not feeling too good.

An amazing effort by all the other guys – Richard for his time of 4 hours and 46 minutes and the other six struggling on with sickness, torn calf muscles and trashed feet. It was great to see everyone back. Nobody in Tent 95 wanted to see anybody else fall by the wayside.

I headed off to the email tent and sent an email home and then managed to have two minutes on the phone to Cherith – it was great to be able to talk, albeit briefly. On return to the tent I had a load of emails to read, the first ones to arrive. I think everyone felt very emotional, and there were a few tears in our eyes – I was so pleased to receive so many encouraging messages from family and friends. It makes such a difference.

I have spent the evening getting as much food into me as possible and ditching everything I feel will not be needed to get my rucksack as light as possible ready for the next few days.

As I started to write this tonight we were unaware of tomorrows' plans. We have just received an absolute bomb shell which has silenced the tent. The 50 mile normal stage planned for tomorrow has been increased to 90K (56.2m) – an unbelievable distance. It seems very harsh – but I guess that's why we are here and I think it is probably the organiser's way of making sure we experience a real challenge after the disappointment of missing the first day. I can and will do it but will have to really pace myself and I guess it is likely to take between 20 and 24 hours so even if I keep going straight through the night it will be after 5am and potentially daylight and 9 am before I get back.

As I write it is 20 to 9 and there is no surprise that we are all getting into our sleeping bags and the whole bivouac has gone quiet.

It is difficult to say how I feel about tomorrow – I just need to get going and to keep going.

CHAPTER SIXTEEN

STAGE 3
ERG ZNAIGUI TO
AFERDOU NSOOALHINE
57 MILES

1ST APRIL 2009 (APRIL FOOL'S DAY)

I tried to get some much needed sleep last night but it was not helped again by the stony uneven ground and the snoring. This time this was not just from my own tent. The tent next to us includes one entrant who apparently has a BMI of about 40 and smokes like a chimney. [He did not finish, but a very determined guy and I think he will be back in a leaner form next year to give it another go.] I woke up and quite genuinely thought that someone had turned on a generator somewhere on the site. It took me quite a while to realise what was actually causing the noise. He woke up the following morning and I heard him ask the others in his tent if he had been snoring and if he had disturbed them! I think the whole bivouac had been disturbed, not just his tent mates.

I woke up at 5.30am and had to move quickly to go to the loo for the first time since we had left the hotel. I deliberately avoided the provided "toilet" facilities and walked on a few yards and performed al fresco. I did not see the inside of the loos but am told that they are awful. A hole in the ground and because of the diarrhoea which so many competitors have been experiencing there are faeces scattered around and this will only increase the number of people who are having problems.

I started to sort out my food and bag in readiness for today (and tomorrow). My plans for today in terms of eating are different to other days. I will obviously need to eat during the time I am out on the trail. However, I do not want to have to stop and get out my stove and fuel tablets and heat up water to rehydrate a main meal. I decided therefore, before leaving England, to have a main meal for breakfast and muesli with skimmed milk to which I would add water shortly before it went dark. This turned out to be a bad move in relationship to my breakfast plans, and one of the few things that I had not trialled before heading out here. I can normally tolerate most food and have tried Expedition chilli con carne before which was my chosen meal for today. However, eating it at 6.30 in the morning in the Sahara after a disturbed night is totally different to eating it during the day at home and I could not get all 800 calories inside me.

At 6.30a.m. to shouts of "Y'allah, Y'allah" the berbers arrived and within seconds the tent had been collapsed around us. It doesn't matter what you are doing at the time – the tent just disappears and shortly after the blanket on the floor follows. This would normally have happened every morning and I guess we are fortunate that because of the rescheduled course this is the first time we have experienced this procedure. We are also fortunate in that this morning it was sunny and warm and so we weren't left exposed and cold.

After a quick tidy up, throwing away any rubbish and anything not absolutely required it was time to load up my rucksack. I was using my Garmin watch to act both as a timer and also with its GPS to record the distance I was covering each day. As the battery only works for about ten hours I had it attached to my Solio charger and taped to its own charging device and then attached to the front of my rucksack. I had checked this out before and found it would run for over 35 hours – more than enough time to get back. Unfortunately for reasons I do not understand it failed to live up to expectations during the day and the battery ran out after approximately 13 hours and so for the last few hours while travelling in

16 – STAGE THREE

the dark I was not certain how far I had travelled, what speed I was travelling at or how far I had before the next check-point. Sun cream was applied and water collected and I was ready and raring to go.

I was aware of the size of the challenge ahead but realistically believed it was achievable. I had to stay focused and determined and to remember that I had prepared for this day. I had experienced on numerous training sessions the discomfort and fatigue which tends to hit me at about 28 to 30 miles and I knew that I needed to push on through this and that I then would get my second wind.

I needed to remember that I was using this challenge to raise money for the Happy House Project for the Children of Watamu. These orphaned children face a far greater challenge than the one I was facing and the more sponsorship I could raise by finishing the greater the chance of helping them.

I also latched on to the emails I had received in which a number of people had referred to the fact that they were proud of what I was doing. In particular the one from Cherith – "you are so focused; I am so proud of you". I hadn't thought about it before and it came as a very pleasant and emotional shock to realise that my wife was proud of what I was achieving.

I also was determined not to think about the total distance at any time or the total remaining distance but to tackle the stage in bite size chunks, each bite being the distance to the next check point, distances which I regularly do in training. I was very successful in doing this during the day with the only time that I calculated the remaining distance being at check-point 4 when we had done 31 miles and I remember thinking there was only a marathon left. (Only someone doing an ultra event would be happy that after just over 31 miles there was "only" a marathon left.) The other trick I played during the day today was to try to visualise a training run at home. When I had four miles to the next check-point I visualised it as being one of my training runs with the dogs, to the extent that after one mile I told myself that I had reached the level crossing near home and called Della and BB in order to safely cross the track. I don't think I actually called their names out loud; that may have unsettled other runners near me at the time!

I also reminded myself that in training I had done the Peak District 40 (or 44 miles in my case) which included a lot of climbing and had done that in under eleven hours, that my pack was now lighter than at the start and considerably lighter than the 13kgs (28.5lbs) that I had carried when doing a 38 mile training session at home, and considerably lighter than Ant's pack which had started at 18kgs (nearly 40lbs) and still weighed more than mine did at the start of the whole event.

Before the start of the day we received the route map. I know it was April fool's day but it was at this stage that we discovered that we were not really going to be running just over 56 miles – the total distance was actually 57 miles!

Of all the days for it to happen there was a late start today. Instead of being on the way at 9am we hung around for the normal media event, the singing of happy birthday to those competitors whose birthday it is today and instructions, again all in French with a poor and at times inaudible translation. At last at 9.20am we were off. My intention had been to try to set off doing about 3.5 miles per hour, but I felt very good and very strong and was going closer to 4 miles per hour. I remember being concerned that I would pay for it later.

Shortly into the stage my camera decided to stop functioning. This was so frustrating as I would have no visual record but I did not allow it to unsettle me and indeed it meant that I was not stopping to take photos during the day. I don't think I have been more focussed and determined during a race than I was today. Indeed I have needed to ask other people for details in order to recall some of the route that we travelled.

As we left the camp we travelled on a flat trail which was muddy in patches from all the rain a few days earlier. There was a very strong headwind and I remember thinking of my training in Blackpool on the beach with the strong winds that we experience and how this was paying dividends, mentally and probably also physically.

During the first stage we reached a sandy dunes area, and then some wide open plains. Although there were no obvious houses or villages nearby children appeared as if from nowhere. Although one or two were scrounging from us the majority were quite happy to offer smiles of encouragement and applaud us and to exchange high fives – it seemed very unreal at the time.

As we continued along this section of the trail a young boy emerged herding his flock of ten goats and a little later I saw three very young children sitting at the side of the trail with their flock of twelve goats, apparently miles from anywhere. At the top of one of the small hills that we climbed, again apparently miles from anywhere, a man was sitting doing nothing. I had agonised about socks, shoes and gaiters before setting off to do the Marathon des Sables; he was wearing his flip flops!

I don't recall much about check-point 1 but I do remember seeing Nick and Martin arriving just as I was setting off on the second stage. I also do not have much recall of check-points 2 and 3. I have however been told that a number of the check-points looked like a scene out of MASH with people resting, trying to recover from illness, being treated for dehydration with intravenous fluids being delivered and attending to horrendous blisters and feet with skin separating off. I understand that two entrants had to be evacuated by helicopter, although do not know if this is correct, or one of the many rumours that circulate in this situation.

I eventually reached check-point 4 at 31 miles in almost exactly nine hours. That meant that I was travelling at an average speed of just under 3.5 miles per hour and was making good progress. I was certainly well within the cut off time which was a very generous 16 hours. I stopped in total for 25 minutes, the only significant stop during the whole 57 miles. I had planned to sort myself out ready for the overnight phase at one of the check-points and this was the obvious place to do that as it was just after 6pm and was starting to go dark and cooler.

I found some bin bags full of discarded water bottles which made an excellent seat – much more comfortable than sitting on the ground, and made it easier to get back onto my feet when I was ready to push on again than getting up off the floor. It was getting quite cold and so the first task was to put on my Skins and my merino wool top, the combination of which proved to be effective throughout the rest of the night, although if I had been out much longer I think I would have needed another layer.

I had been using my sunglasses, with an optical insert, and with a sun lens and had to change this for one of the clear lenses for the night stage.

Then it was time for some food. My plan paid dividends here because it took me only one minute to put some water into my food bag containing muesli with nuts and skimmed milk, and it gave me 600 calories. It was probably also easier to eat and digest than a spaghetti bolognese or a chicken tikka!

At check-point 3 I had been given a fluorescent stick and this needed to be bent forcibly to set off the chemical reaction which resulted in it glowing orange before placing it in the back of my rucksack on the outside in order for following competitors to be able to pick out the route being taken by the rest of the field. I was just about to set off when I remembered I had not put my head torch on, and having remedied this I was ready for the next phase of the stage.

I have to admit that this was the part of the race that I was most apprehensive about before setting off from England, and as I left check-point 4 I felt extremely nervous. It was getting dark and I was unsure how easy it would be to navigate my way across the dunes and trails to the subsequent check-points. I made sure I set off just behind some of the other competitors, although they were setting a fairly rapid pace and I realised that I would have to try to keep a good speed going if I was not to fall behind. Initially I found navigation quite difficult as we were heading through another area of sand dunes and direct routes were not possible.

The system for navigation relies on the marker posts that are placed approximately a third of a mile apart. At night these are illuminated by a fluorescent stick similar to that in each entrants rucksack but glowing a green colour. The idea is to head from one green stick to another and of course to follow the orange fluorescent sticks of other competitors. It took a while but eventually I got my orientation and got the hang of the system and my apprehension lessened and eventually disappeared.

As we came out of the sand dunes and onto a level trail it was clear that there was a progression of orange sticks ahead which were going uphill. Just what I wanted after over 32 miles, particularly as from a distance it looked very steep. I think if I had known what was ahead I would have been more than a little dubious.

On arrival at the start of the climb it was apparent that we had to work our way up a very steep rocky crevasse. It involved a lot of hard work as we all in line climbed, scrambled and almost crawled our way slowly upwards with a lot of encouragement and assistance from our fellow competitors. I am not exactly sure how much climbing was involved and it was probably no more than about 350 feet [a check on my Garmin watch on return suggests it was about 500 feet] but in the dark and after 32 miles it was very tough and very slow and like most of the others involved I do not mind admitting, now that I have completed the stage, that I was frightened at times.

The ascent was merely a prelude to what was to come when we reached the top. There were no clear markings and I am still not sure if we went the correct way to reach the top but think we did, although some of those around me felt that we should have branched off part way up the climb. As we accessed the ridge at the top there were no clear markings to indicate where we went next. As we looked to our right there was however a clear long line of fluorescent orange sticks and so the next stage was clear.

The problem was how to get from the top of the climb to the trail that obviously now awaited us. There was in fact an equally difficult and frightening descent. I have always been more nervous about going downhill than uphill after a nasty fall and injury to my knee as a teenager. There was no clear path and we had to work our way down a rocky area with patches of slippery sand. I was very relieved to reach the trail path at the bottom.

A lot of time had been taken on a very small distance but it was now possible to move on along a trail path and the route was very clear as there were so many others in close proximity. The path led into a set of very steep sand hills. I remember as we travelled along in the dark with very little moonlight thinking that it was a bit like being on the ski slopes although unfortunately no ski lifts or downhill descents for shooshing down. I also seemed to be spending a lot of time off-piste and recall one particularly steep sand hill. I assume that there was a ridge along the top of it but we did not see it in the dark and worked our way along the side of it. Finding it difficult to maintain a footing I was sliding progressively downwards and had to work hard to get back to the top again and make onward progress.

As I approached check-point 5 I realised that the stretch from check-point 4 to check-point 5 had taken a lot out of me and I was beginning to struggle. I had to make a decision. I could stop and rest and partially recover, but this would mean losing time. Alternatively I could keep pushing on but I was aware that I would then be away from any check-points for a further nine miles if I ran into any problems, something I wanted to obviously avoid in the dark.

I stopped for about five to ten minutes to get some energy bars into me and get my head together and then made a decision to push on and go for it. I refused to allow myself to think of anything but the distance I had to cover to check-point 6, approximately 9 miles, and not to calculate or consider the total distance to the finish, some 17 miles. I did however encourage myself with the thought that when I reached the next check-point I only had one final stage to go to the end of the 57 miles.

I cannot recall much of the next part of the trail and cannot remember if it was just stony trail or if there were any sand dunes. I do recall that my torch was woefully inadequate – the only piece of equipment that I was not happy with. In the darkness I missed a bush on the trail, until I fell into it. I came up with my usual good fortune smelling not of roses, but of lavender! The sweetest smell that I was associated with for the full six days.

I also remember that the person in front of me suddenly came across a herd of camels across the track that had not been noticeable in the dark. The camels scattered to either side of the trail and I recall hoping that he had not separated a mother from its calf and that as a result my Marathon des Sables might come to a premature end as mother rushed back to protect its young.

It was also between these two check-points that my watch failed and so I could not be sure how fast I was going or how far I had to go to the next check-point. I also had a normal watch with me so with some difficulty because of my poor head light I was able to check what time it was. I recall that at times I would look at my watch and find it was only a few minutes since my last check and that time seemed to be standing still, and other occasions when 30 or 40 minutes seemed to pass by in a flash.

Check-point 6 was illuminated by a laser beam which was shining upwards from the ground. This seemed to be playing cruel tricks. It seemed an inordinate distance to the point where the beam started and it looked impossible that we were going to have to travel so far to reach it. Then as we rounded a curve the intensity of the beam suddenly appeared to increase dramatically and it was clear that there was not as far to travel as I had thought. But this was where the second cruel trick revealed itself because no matter how much I pushed on it appeared to still be the same distance away. It reminded me of climbing the sand dunes and heading back to camp on the second day.

It was a relief to reach the check-point and the realisation that there was just the final phase to complete. I stopped for long enough to eat another energy bar, check my feet and top up my water. The other competitor in front of me who had disturbed the camels was sorting himself out adjacent to where I was standing. I suggested to him that it might be a good idea to do the final miles together. It was certainly a good idea as far as I was concerned and it was obvious to me that he was also relieved to have company. I remember him saying that he was not worried about the pace but we would just stick together.

I had no preconceived intention for this stage but suddenly found that we were going at a cracking pace and certainly much quicker than if I had been struggling down on my own. I will always be grateful to Paul, a police diver from Australia, for his mutual support. Although an Australian he is from Scotland and after the event was heading back to Scotland to see his family. It was obvious he was missing his wife and young children who were still in Australia.

I was not only glad for Paul's company but also for his head torch.

The final section, into a strong wind, was a very stony trail and a number of other people did serious damage to their feet on this part of the course and will end up losing toe nails from the bruising they sustained. If I had been on my own with my own head torch I am fairly certain that I would have missed a lot of the large stones and would potentially have not only damaged my feet but also have fallen over a number of times.

Paul and I actually speeded up over this final stage and covered 7.25 miles in less than two hours – not bad at the end of 57 miles! Once again the camp site appeared, but then never seemed to get any closer. It would have been demoralising if I had been on my own. I eventually crossed the finish line in a time of 17 hours 56 minutes and 36 seconds and in 362nd position, a huge improvement on previous days.

It was difficult to find the tent in the dark as we were at a new site and it took some time to work out the arrangement of the tents. Richard had correctly suggested that it was important that we each tried to get some food inside us on return and I had indeed planned for this. He also suggested that as he would probably be the first back he would leave his stove, pot and water together with some fuel tablets for the next person in, who would do the same for the person behind. Richard also suggested that the first one in should move to the back of the tent so that others could get in without disturbing those already back. Brilliant in theory!

When I found the tent there was a body sprawled in the entrance to the tent, lying at 90 degrees to our normal sleeping position. It was Richard; and there was no water or fuel waiting for me. Like me he was exhausted and had just collapsed into his sleeping bag in the entrance to the tent. I put my rucksack down and sank onto my hands and knees to get out my sleeping bag and thermarest. Having got into that position I was unable to get upright again, and so like Richard I had nothing to eat and lay down to try to sleep where I had knelt down.

I think the ground surface on which I was lying was the most uncomfortable that we experienced all the time. I was obviously lying on hard stones and rocks. It almost appeared as if they had deliberately sought out the most uncomfortable patch of ground and to make it worse had brought some extra stones off the trail we had just been on and spread them round the tent!

Despite my exhaustion I was not able to sleep. This was in part because of the ground but also because my legs were so uncomfortable. I took two Paracetamol (the first time I have needed to touch my medical kit) and dosed fitfully for a few hours. By about 7am I was up and moving around and trying to get some fluids and food back on board.

2ND APRIL 2009

I started the day with a phone call to Cherith. Once again I felt very emotional and was not able to talk much but good to hear her voice and I am sure she was relieved to know that I was OK. She already knew that I had finished because Alistair (my son) has been keeping an eye on the official web site and had been able to find out that I had crossed the finishing line.

The aim of getting yesterday finished in one go was so that I could have a really good rest day today before the final two stages of a marathon and then a 10 to 12 mile final stage. Unfortunately we were advised at the start yesterday that the final stage has had to be cancelled. It is a pity that we were not given an explanation as this only encourages rumours and potential dissatisfaction.

I am not sure why this has happened. One realistic explanation relates to the route planners who put out the markers. The routes are understandably planned a number of months in advance. The organisers have done an amazing job in putting on the event that we have had in the circumstances. It has however involved them flying over the potential course to check for good ground and safety. They have then had to go out and mark the new course. They have been working flat out and must be exhausted and apparently there is concern for them and their safety and also about the potential for mistakes in marking the course. I am not sure if this is the correct explanation but whatever the reason there is only the marathon stage left.

My plan has paid off because I have managed to spend most of today resting. I have not really slept but have pottered around, eaten as much as possible to recharge the batteries, chatted to various people and taken some photos around the camp site using Rob's camera which he has kindly lent to me.

I also was delighted to welcome the rest of the tent as they have reappeared. It was good to see them all with their various tales and to know that the whole tent is still in the race. It would be awful if anyone missed out, particularly at this stage, and would have had a dampening effect on the whole tent. There were times as the day went on when I was concerned but eventually at approximately 3.20pm Joe and Ant arrived having been out on the trail for a fraction over 30 hours. In many ways it is much harder for those finishing at this stage. Not only are they out on the trail for much longer each day, although with no more water, but they also have less rest time in which to recover. I had managed to laze around for 12 hours before they got back to the tent.

Joe and Ant had taken the opportunity to have a number of rests at various check-points and get a rather disturbed sleep. They had both been having trouble with blisters. Joe has a particularly painful foot which is probably due to bruising from the constant pounding on hard, stony trails and Ant has been unwell with diarrhoea. They have both done really well. Apparently shortly after leaving check-point 4 they came across an American female who had got lost and had climbed into her sleeping bag to wait for daylight. They helped her along over the next stage and appear to have acted as support, guide and counsellors to a number of other waifs and strays.

Nick and Martin had been the first to follow me back into our tent at about 8.00am in a time of 22 hours and 27 minutes. Again they had both done a great job, Nick suffering from bad blisters and Martin with diarrhoea and vomiting. Later in the day Martin looked like death warmed up and was obviously dehydrated and struggling to get much needed food into him.

Russell was the next to appear and on his own at nearly 12.30pm after 27 hours and 3 minutes. This stage appears to have been a really negative experience for him and he is struggling physically and mentally. He had left Rob after check-point 3 and had been on his own for the rest of the stage. He had struggled up the rocky crevasse after check-point 4 with virtually no one else around at about 3 in the morning and unable to see any marker signs or any other competitors he had continued to travel in the same direction as he descended rather than turning to his right. It would appear that the organisers saw his orange fluorescent stick and were able to redirect him. In addition he was struggling with blisters and the front zip on his gaiters was malfunctioning. They needed to be held together with gaffer tape for the rest of the event. Later on in the day he went down with a bout of diarrhoea.

Rob returned between Russell, and Joe and Ant at about 2pm in a time of 28 hours and 47 minutes. He had really suffered between stages 3 and 4 and had taken the opportunity to have a rest and sleep at check-point 4 before carrying on to finish the stage. He also had blistered feet.

During the day as I looked around the camp it was a bizarre sight to see so many people hobbling around with trashed feet. It appears that far more people have problems than are OK. Many people are using their trekking poles to gingerly move around and some are on crutches. It is perfectly clear that all intend to continue. There is a general feeling that you just don't pack in on this event no matter what you are going through. I feel almost embarrassed that I have absolutely no problems. I have no signs of any blisters and no stomach upset. Richard is also doing very well with just one small blister. I am sure that there is an element that I have been lucky. However I think there are a number of other factors which account for how I am at this stage.

- I decided the socks that I was going to wear along with the shoes and gaiters a number of months ago and have been using them regularly ever since.
- I have done a lot of walking as part of my training. Much of this event involves walking and there is no doubt that the action is very different from running with different forces applied to the soles of the feet.

- I have done most of my training on trails rather than on hard pavements, and a lot in Tenerife where the paths with volcanic stones are very similar to those here in the Sahara.
- I have elevated my feet every night when returning from the stage.
- I have kept myself well hydrated and have got all my planned calories in.
- I have only eaten foods, gels and bars that I have tried before and which I know don't upset me.
- I have not used the toilet facilities provided by the organisers which I am sure are helping to spread the diarrhoea and vomiting which so many are experiencing.

At approximately 8pm the last two competitors arrived back having been out on the trail for about 35 hours, and closely followed in by the camel. The whole camp turned out for the traditional welcome in of the final competitors who were surrounded by a media scrum.

Not quite 9pm and once again it is time to turn in for some sleep. We have been told that the marathon stage tomorrow is going to include some tough hills – a final sting in the tail. One stage left and I am still feeling OK and expect to finish. It would take a major disaster to stop me now. I just have to hope that I do not get hit with diarrhoea or pick up an injury.

CHAPTER SEVENTEEN

STAGE 4
AFERDOU NSOOUALHINE
TO TIZIN IGRS
26.2 MILES

3RD APRIL 2009

I actually slept quite well last night; certainly the best since I have been in the tent. I still woke at about 5.30am as it was starting to get light. I was soon out of my sleeping bag for the usual routine which I have now got used to. It was good to know that breakfast today will be my last self sufficiency meal and as I had planned muesli and skimmed milk I did not need to heat up any water or eat any more of the dehydrated food.

Our tents and blankets disappeared shortly after 6am and by 8.30am we were ready to go. We had to wait for the now all too familiar announcements and singing of happy birthday. At 9am we were on the way for the final time.

I knew that I needed to stay focussed for just a few more hours. My main aim was to get to the finish line, but I wanted to do some more running and as I had improved my stage position and overall position each day I was hoping it would be possible to keep the trend going for the final day.

I set off along a long, straight and level stony trail at a jogging pace with the intention of running for eight minutes and walking for two on level ground, while walking any uphill sections or very sandy areas. My plan worked well initially. Then I reached a particularly difficult hill and I took my time walking up it and having a good look around me at the impressive hills in the distance in all directions. It took almost ten minutes to reach the top although admittedly I had to stop for some photographs. As I descended the other side and had almost reached the level trail again I managed to slip and ended up on the ground. No damage done but a warning to be careful.

I reached check-point 1 at the end of a raised area and had my usual quick stopover before pushing on. It was not long before the trail gave way to sandy areas, some mud patches and then sand hills and so I stopped any attempt at jogging and carried on with my usual speed walking. Suddenly I was at check-point 2 at the end of a raised area and I knew that I only had one final section to go before the last ever check point.

Leaving check-point 2 I travelled along a stony trail with muddy and sandy areas before entering a further stretch of sand hills. I realised that as I walked through the final stretch of these dunes that I was close to check-point 3. I also realised from the road map that this was the final stretch of dunes for the whole event. I slowed down and deliberately had a good look around to take it all in for one last time. The dunes had been tough but for me had been the most beautiful part of the journey. I knew it was unlikely that I would ever be back in the Sahara and I wanted to be able to remember this spectacular area and stunning scenery.

As we left check-point 3 for the final journey to the finishing line we made an acute turn onto a stony trail. It had been my intention to run as much as possible of this final stretch but I was also aware that my energy levels were for some reason low and I was also aware of a vague discomfort in my right knee. I wanted to make sure that I got to the finish line and if possible ran across it and so I decided not to risk anything and continued to walk.

We had been warned that during this final stage there was a wadi with water across the trail and had also been advised that we had to

17 – STAGE FOUR

follow the route markers which meant we had to go through the water. I was later told that if we had carried on a little along the trail we could have gone across on dry ground – but the point of the Marathon des Sables is to make it tough so that was never going to be an option. As I approached the water I could see a number of children playing in it. I stopped to take a photograph and immediately they rushed towards me to pose for the picture and then held out their hands for bon-bons! My final few jelly babies were put to good use.

I met a number of other children along the final few miles, mainly offering encouragement and high fives, but some obviously looking for anything I had to give away. As on previous days I have no idea where they had emerged from.

On this final stretch I was told on a number of occasions the distance to the finish, from photographers and local children. All their estimates were wrong and were under estimates!

I had realised by now that there are always a few tricks that the organisers play to make a tough challenge even tougher. No surprises today because just three or four miles from the finish there was a long slow uphill trail. I kept pushing on and reached the top and it was no surprise to discover that in front of me there was another short level stretch followed by another long gradual uphill section. I just needed to keep plodding on and keep focussed.

As I reached the top of this incline the markers pointed us to the left and as I looked over the top of the ridge I could see in the far off distance the welcome sight of the inflatables and the finish line for the 24th Marathon des Sables. But all was not finished because after another 100 yards we had to turn right and go downhill and for the first time in the whole event there were officials waiting to help us down over a very steep, slippery sand patch.

The final run in must be the longest finishing line ever in any event. Having reached the trail it must have been well over a mile to the finish. I broke into a slow jog for approximately half of the distance and then a period of walking. With the finish line in sight and knowing that I could run the remaining distance I broke into my last run and with my arms raised in the air I crossed the finish line in just under seven hours for the marathon and a total running time of 37 hours 54 minutes and 53 seconds for the whole event. I received my medal and the traditional kiss from Patrick Bauer, the race director, and then again raised my arms and looking directly into the web cam let rip a hearty scream of success. I did not know it at the time but Alistair was watching on his computer as I crossed the line.

I had finished the 24th Marathon des Sables and despite my earlier concerns that the abbreviated event would make me feel as though I had not done a true Marathon des Sables I had a huge sense of satisfaction and achievement. In some ways this year has been harder rather than easier; the total distance at 125 miles is lower than normal but this has been over four days and not the traditional six days and the long day is the longest stage there has ever been, and the longest there is ever likely to be in the future.

I did not feel as emotional as I expected and later in discussion realised that the others in my tent felt the same way. I am sure that this will come when we eventually get home to our friends and families. In the meantime, of course, everyone around us has achieved the same success and it doesn't seem anything unusual.

It was odd to have finished "the toughest foot race on earth" in 449th position and in 49th position out of 103 for my age group (men age 50 to 60) despite the fact that next year I will move out of this age group and yet still feel a twinge of disappointment. Not disappointment that the event was over, but with my performance on the last day. I had improved my position and overall position every day until today and had been hoping to maintain progress. I thought I had been doing well and was surprised to find that I was in a lower position than expected. No need to be ashamed and no need to worry because no one else is particularly interested in my position, just the fact that I have completed this event.

For the final day I was again the second back from Tent 95 and I was followed back very shortly by Rob who had had the best day of the event, and I think was a little disappointed that he had not pushed himself

17 – STAGE FOUR

harder on the previous days. His time of 7 hours 14 minutes and 51 seconds was a great improvement on his previous days and a great achievement for someone who does not consider himself a runner and had only been running because he wanted to take up the challenge of this amazing event.

Richard, Rob and I went for a walk up the hill at the back of the camp as we were told this was a rich area for finding fossils up to 350 million years old. We saw some interesting fossils, as well as a magnificent view from the top, but decided it was wrong to remove the fossils and bring any home with us. Despite this we were approached by a number of locals trying to persuade us to buy fossils and trinkets. We declined.

Nick, Martin and Russell all crossed the finishing line together in a time of 9 hours and 11 minutes and I think were relieved to get to the end of their journey, particularly after the problems they had all faced. The final two back were Ant and Joe in a time of 10 hours 6 minutes and 47 seconds. As Ant and Joe saw the finishing line after the final climb and with over a mile still to go one of the reasons for the weight in Ant's rucksack was revealed. He produced a 1 litre bottle of rum and topped up his and Joe's water bottle with a lethally strong mixture. They are possibly the first, and only, contestants to cross the finishing line of the Marathon des Sables with high blood alcohol levels!

Not only had we reached the end of the Marathon des Sables but we had also reached the end of the requirement for self sufficiency. We joined yet another queue for dinner in the restaurant set up in the desert. It was marvellous to eat proper food again – soup, spaghetti bolognese, carrots (cold and fresh) followed by bread and cheese, fruit salad and cake. And it was all helped down with a bottle of wine. The only problem for me was sitting on the floor at a very low table and the difficulty in sitting comfortably and in particular of getting back onto my feet again.

The evening ended the whole event in a memorable fashion with an outdoor concert. A stage had been set up and illuminated and approximately 25 members of the Paris Opera entertained us while sitting on the floor in the Sahara desert with a star lit sky above our heads. Music from Schindler's List, Blue Danube, Strauss and Handel and then a performance of Gershwin's Summer Time. Although I heard some people being critical – some people are never satisfied – I felt that the choice of music was just right for the circumstances and for the audience who were perhaps not normally attendees at classical music concerts. There cannot be many people who have set on the ground in the Sahara under a star lit sky and heard a concert delivered by professional musicians.

And after the concert it was off to bed for the final time in the desert at about 10pm with two Paracetamol for my aching legs. It is great to think that tomorrow night I will be in a bed, with a pillow and I will have had a shower and a shave.

CHAPTER EIGHTEEN

RETURN TO NORMALITY – IN STAGES

4ST APRIL 2009

I had a bad night again last night. First of all my legs were really uncomfortable and I had to take a further two Paracetamol, although not bad as during the whole time we have been here I have only taken six Paracetamol and no other tablets. I also got up during the night and went and had a wash! My legs were so sticky from days of running and sweating without a proper wash and I just felt so unpleasant. It was good to step outside and use my last wet ones and soap leaves and remove some of the accumulated sweat and dirt.

Last night I gave some of my supply of Ciprofloxacin, used for traveller's diarrhoea, to three of the guys in my tent. I am not going to need them now and they all have a problem. They are also taking Imodium. Despite the treatment, one, who shall be nameless, had to get up several times during the night and is now without a pair of Helly Hansen trousers! Not as bad as one of the competitors who has had so many problems that he has had to cut up his night clothing to use as toilet paper!

At 6.30am Rob Long, the robotic tour guide from The Best of

Morocco, visited our tent and in his monotone voice advised us that the British were to be the last to leave camp and that the coaches would leave at approximately 11am for a five to six hour journey back to Ouarzazete. It was to prove to be a long day.

We joined the all too familiar queue which appears to characterise this event for breakfast. I have not added up the total time we spent queuing but think it must be close to the total taken to complete the 125 miles. Again it was great to have a good breakfast with proper food – juice, cereal, ham, fried eggs, bread, cheese, honey, coffee and tea.

In the queue behind us was Mohammed Ahansal, the winner of the event. I cannot imagine Paula Radcliffe joining a queue for her breakfast with all the other entrants of the London Marathon. That is not a personal criticism of any individual but a reflection of the type of event that I have just completed. Also in the queue was a blind competitor who had been guided around the course. That is beyond my understanding. As we sat down outside to eat our breakfast we were sitting at the next table to Patrick Bauer, the race director. There cannot be many events where a blind competitor, the winner along with middle to end of the pack runners queue together for their food and then sit down to eat with the race director. There is total respect from everyone for everyone else and there are no prima donnas.

Eventually we set off at about midday and as we travelled back via couch through Erfoud, the town to which we had been evacuated one week earlier, the road signs told us that we had just over 185 miles to travel. It was a slow journey because of the need for frequent toilet stops and despite the 100 Dirham (just under £8) bribe that Ant offered the driver to be the first of our six coaches back we were not able to break away from the strictly controlled convoy in which we travelled.

We arrived back at the Berber Palace Hotel, in Ouarzazete, to join yet another queue for our room key. Our luggage had been returned to the hotel earlier that week. As a final test we were told that it was on the first floor with no lift access.

It was good to get back to the rooms we had been in the previous week and to get out of clothes which we had been wearing all the time for six days. I am not sure if they will ever recover. I scraped away at six days of stubble and then stepped into a hot shower to remove the first layer of dirt. Once that had been done it was possible to lie down in a bath and have a good soak.

The first beer of the evening tasted like nectar and then for some food while sitting outside. Russell was struggling and had collapsed on his bed. Before heading downstairs I had persuaded him to get a shower and then took some food up to him because he could not face the restaurant. When I headed back to my room at about 9.30pm he had managed to eat something and was starting to rally around.

5TH APRIL 2009

Despite the opportunity of a lie in I was awake by 7.00am and after reading my book for a while was out of bed by 7.30am and feeling much better for a sleep in a bed with sheets and a pillow. Russell was feeling much better after a good night's sleep and was ready to celebrate his birthday.

Following a breakfast of cereal, omelette, bacon, bread and coffee in the hotel restaurant we headed to the hotel where the finisher's T shirts were available. We had got used to queuing but this was the queue to end all queues and it took well over an hour to get into the room where the shirts were available and where other merchandise could be purchased.

There appeared to be a bizarre system for purchasing and paying for everything but we had to go with the process. I bought the book of the Marathon des Sables as well as a few clothes and of course collected my finisher's T-shirt; I had worked and sweated for it and was not going to leave that behind. As we sat outside we met one of the competitors in the first ever Marathon des Sables who signed my book adjacent to his photograph with the first 25 runners in 1986. We noticed that at one of the other tables was Mohammed Ahansal, and Richard, who had also bought the book, and I thought it would be a good idea to have his signature at the front of our books. We approached him and offered our congratulations and then Richard asked for his signature. He happily signed the book and it was as he was signing and wrote "2nd in 24th Marathon des Sables" that we realised we had made a mistake. A simple case of mistaken identity. I quietly moved away!

We returned our purchases to our hotel before setting off for the hole in the wall, which was not churning out money for most of our cards, and then on to a leisurely lunch of beef kebab and chips– at a forced leisurely pace as service was at Moroccan speed. We decided to visit the Kasbah but as we got near to the entrance we were approached by a local merchant who encouraged us to visit his store and that of others in the area behind the Kasbah. It was a fascinating insight into the local way of life and there is no way any of us would have gone down the poverty stricken alleys if we had been on our own. We kept a constant look out to make sure we were all together. At one point we came across a group who were obviously completely stoned out of their minds. Our friendly guide pushed them to one side and we moved on.

The shops included the normal tourist type shops selling clothes, ceramic plates, jewellery and camels as well as food shops and an herbalist's shop which was very colourful. (I use the word "shop" in a very loose sense.) At one point in an open area there were a number of local ladies washing their clothes in a number of plastic tubs. As we approached the end of the area and were heading out we were encouraged to stop at a house where there was a lady with a very young child. We looked in to see one tiny dishevelled room, cluttered with what appeared to be rubbish. It is difficult to imagine how it is possible to live in such conditions – I think our tents of the last six days have been more spacious and comfortable. The final sight was a house with a number of well painted ladies leaning out of the windows. We decided that this was not somewhere to stop or to take a photograph.

A number of those in the tent felt they would like to try a hammam – like a steam room with water provided to wash yourself. We had made enquiries and knew where we could find a local facility. One of our guides wearing his white trousers and yellow slip on shoes accompanied us on his moped. We seemed to be heading into an even more squalid area. When we arrived we were told we had to leave everything outside. Absolutely no

18 – RETURNING TO NORMALITY

chance. We asked to look around inside. It was like a scene out of Dante's inferno and the associated smell was far worse than anything we had experienced in the bivouacs over the previous six days.

As we walked from one steamy and hot room to another we were horrified. A young boy, no more than about six years of age, was lying motionless in the first room in a recovery type position. In other rooms there were boys of various ages and adult men, some wearing loin cloths and some naked. This was most definitely not what we were looking for and we made a hasty retreat and headed back to the hotel, in a taxi with a shattered front window, no speedometer and a screw to open and close the door, for a hammam and massage for a few of the tent in the hygienic and safe surroundings of a 5 star hotel.

Following a shower I packed everything together as there was an early start the next day and headed down for another meal and a few beers. I was in bed once again by 10pm. It will be a long day tomorrow, but like everyone else I just want to get home again now. It will be good to see Cherith and my family and the dogs and sleep in my own bed.

6TH APRIL 2009

Had to leave the hotel this morning at 6am and so set my alarm for 5am, remembering on this occasion that my phone was set to British Summer Time. There was actually no need to set my alarm as I was woken by the call to prayers just before 5am.

The coach left the hotel after breakfast shortly after 6am for the five to ten minute journey to the airport. Ours was the only flight being boarded and we were probably about two thirds of the way down the queue when we initially joined it. Despite the flight being due to leave at 8am we were only just checking in at that time. The queue to end all queues, which I thought we had been in the previous day, was a poor imitation of a real queue. I hate to think what would happen if there were two planes going at the same time.

We had a really good flight back and Russell treated himself to champagne – I think he must be feeling better. We were back at Gatwick at around 1pm. If I thought queues were a Moroccan specialty then I was mistaken as we then joined a long and painfully slow queue for passport control and finally another one to reclaim our luggage, minus Martin's trail pole.

It was an emotional moment as we said goodbye to each other form Tent 95. Eight strangers just ten days ago had become good friends who had shared a never to be forgotten experience. There had been the potential for conflict and disagreement but instead we had experienced nothing but harmony, laughter and a great deal of support. We had become a team and it was sad to say farewell, although I have no doubt it will not be long before we meet up again.

I reversed my journey of twelve days previously via Victoria, Euston and Preston railway stations before arriving at Poulton-le-Fylde in the rain just before 7pm. It was so good to see Cherith again, to arrive back home, to sit down with my favourite tipple – a glass of Jamesons and to talk and share experiences.

My journey which started on 20th April 2006 had indeed come to a highly satisfactory conclusion.

CHAPTER NINETEEN

THE ROUTE MAPS

Km 0 : Go South (180°) to reach start of dunes.
Km 1.7: Enter dunes. Take bearing 159° to cross Erg Chebbi.
Km 14.5: CP1 at end of dunes. Go S/SW (bearing 198°), going alongside vegetation on edge of wadi.
Km 16.3: Cross wadi.
Km 17: Exit wadi. Stoney ground. Go South (187°) until CP2
Km 18.1: Sand and small dunes in wadi.
Km 19.8: End of Min'Ajer wadi. Stoney ground.
Km 20.1: Cross track. Merdani village is a few hundred metres on your right. Stoney ground, ± undulating until CP2.
Km 23.2: First ruins of MFis village.
Km 23.8: CP2. Cross stoney valley, heading South to reach sandy passage through jebel Debouaâ.
Km 25.5: Small hill.
Km 25.9: Small sandy pass in Debouaâ jebel.
Km 26.1: End of pass. Cross valley.
Km 26.7: End of valley. Follow branch of wadi that goes up the small hill.
Km 27 : Aim left, then right. Cross stoney plateau.
Km 27.8: Follow wadi bed in middle of small gorge that descends between small hills.
Km 29.2: End of gorge. Follow branch of wadi that goes slightly to the left.
Km 29.9: Beginning of erg Znaïgui dunes. Take bearing 138° until B3.
Km 33 : Arrive at B3, at end of dunes

<u>**STAGE 1**</u>   30 March 2009 - Erg Chebbi/Erg Znaïgui : 19.5 miles

Conditions at 10am: 20 degrees C and 36% humidity
Conditions at 1.30pm: 29 degrees C and 24% humidity

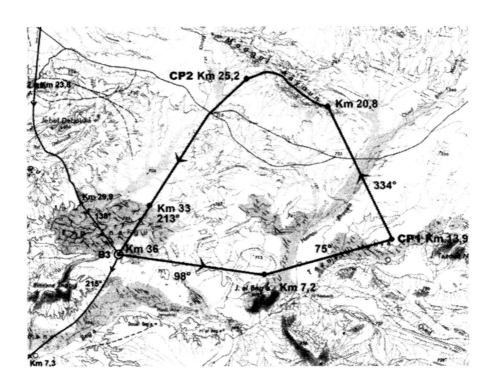

STAGE 2   31/03/09 - Erg Znaïgui/Erg Znaïgui : 22 miles

Conditions at 8.45am: 15.8 degrees C and 38% humidity

Conditions at 10am: 20.7 degrees C and 37% humidity

Conditions at 12.15pm: 24 degrees C and 18% humidity

6 retirements at 12.15pm

19 – ROUTE MAPS

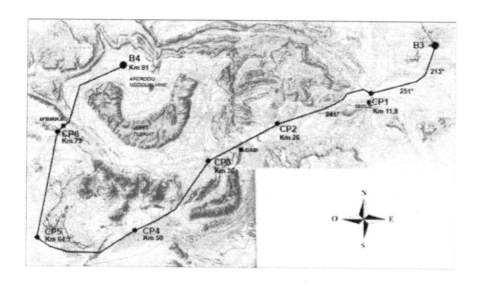

STAGE 3   01/04/09 – Erg Znaïgui/Aferdou Nsooualhine: 57 miles

Conditions at 9.15am: 20 degrees C and 36% humidity

Conditions at 1pm: 29 degrees C and 29% humidity

13 retirements at 12.15pm

02/04/09

Conditions at 9.30am: 31 degrees C and 31% humidity

Conditions at 12.15pm: 29 degrees C and 24.7% humidity

33 retirements at 9.30am

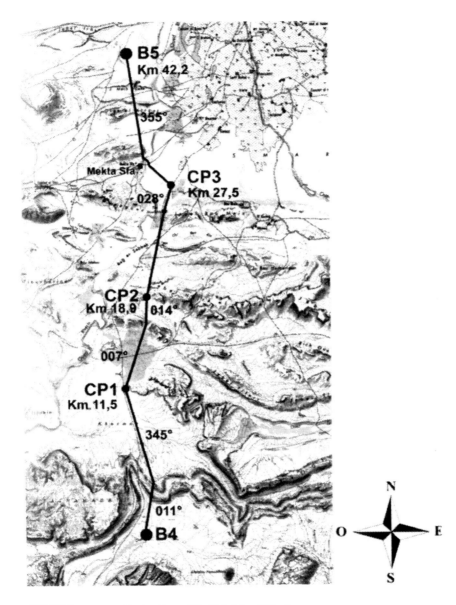

STAGE 4 03/04/09 - Aferdou Nsooualhine/Tizin Ighrs: 26.2 miles

Conditions at 9.45am: 21.4 degrees C and 29.6% humidity
Conditions at 12.15pm: 29 degrees C and 16.5% humidity

19 – ROUTE MAPS

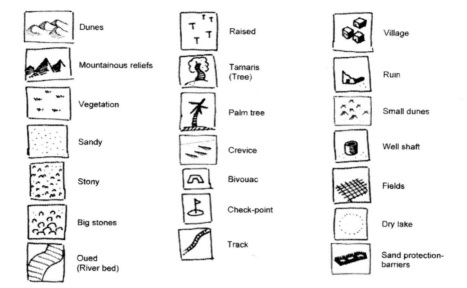

PART SIX

MY CHOSEN CHARITY
THE HAPPY HOUSE PROJECT
THE CHILDREN OF WATAMU

CHAPTER TWENTY

RAISING MONEY FOR CHARITY

The Marathon des Sables is not a charity event, but I as well as many others used the opportunity to raise money for charity. I have managed to raise approximately £8,000 and Tent 95 together has raised over £40,000. If this is typical then, with over 100 tents this year the total raised for charity is likely to be in the region of £400,000.

When I ran the Antarctic Ice Marathon I had raised money for Cancer Research UK and was able to hand over a cheque for over £30,000. I have absolutely no doubt that this money was well used. However, I could not personally see the impact it had made. I decided on this occasion to ask my sponsors to support a smaller charity where I and they could see the impact that their money was making. I chose The Happy House Project for The Children of Watamu in Kenya. (www.childrenofwatamu.net)

The story of this charity can best be told by Sue Hayward who with her husband founded this charity. The following information is taken from the charity web site.

"In January 2000, myself and my husband Dave visited a school in Watamu; a small coastal village in Kenya, East Africa. What we saw there were children sitting on cold stone floors in old broken buildings, counting with stones.

We just couldn't believe that this was the year 2000, and children were being educated in these conditions.

Teachers had the nigh impossible task of trying to teach without pencils, papers or books.

On that first visit, Rose Ziro, then headmistress at the school, told us that desks and chairs were the main priority. During that visit we managed to have 36 desks and chairs made for 36 of the 130 children then attending the school.

We travelled about 25 miles to the nearest town to purchase exercise books, paper, pencils and other items just to make a teacher's job possible.

We came home on fire! We could not leave things as they were; we just had to help these children. I believed then as I do now that education is the road out of poverty for these children.

In July 2003 I established Working for the Children of Watamu as a registered charity. Trustees were appointed and we were now well and truly on our way.

By the end of 2003 each of the 130 children had a desk and chair; we even had 20 extras for additional recruits! We did not have to wait long. To cater for the additional children new classrooms were built and many of the old ones refurbished, and the school now caters for 700 children.

From the outset, one of our great aims was to open a Library. Due to the fantastic support of so many people this ambition was fulfilled and the Library now contains over 15,000 books.

A follow-on ambition was to provide a Computer Room and this aim has also been achieved.

We built the 5 classrooms needed for the Secondary School in March 2007.

By January 2008 we had 700 children in full time education, their ages ranging from 2 years to 16.

We feel now that the education side of our work is very well supported. Our next main project has to be to build a Happy House. Some people call these places Orphanages, but to us that would conjure up pictures of a Charles Dickens novel, where cold, dirty, frightened children huddle together.

We don't want this. We want Happy Kids. Ours will be a real Happy home for these children. If you stand outside you will hear laughter and singing. When you enter there will be happy, healthy, smiling faces.

Watamu and the surrounding areas now has a very high number of orphans, due to Aids, malaria and many other diseases that these people have to contend with on a day to day basis. Numerous children are abandoned. Brothers and sisters try to care for each other. Some are not much older than the children they are caring for. Children have disappeared from the village. If a child anywhere in the world goes missing it is headline news. In Watamu a child goes missing, "Well it was an orphan". Where have the kids gone? Where are these children? Are they still alive?

We need a place where these children can live happily in safety. Where they can grow and be children. A place where children can go to sleep in a bed and wake up to a breakfast.

In June 2007 a man well known to us, Grandpa Yaa, very generously donated to the charity four acres of his own land. Grandpa Yaa is 90 years old and lives with his wife Peninah. They married in 1944 have 12 children, 60 grandchildren and 20 great grandchildren. One of his grandson's is Silas, Headmaster of the Primary school.

When Grandpa heard that Sue needed land to build the Happy House, he said to his sons "The land belongs to Kenya, the orphans belong to Kenya, we should give some land to Sue as she is the one that will make a difference to the lives of these unfortunate children". It was a very humbling experience. A 99 year lease was signed.

So now we have the land and we definitely have the kids. The plans have been drawn and passed in February 2008, to accommodate 76 children. The land has been fenced off. A well has been sunk, ready to supply water for the gardens and the building work. A lot of fruit trees have been planted. In time we will be self sufficient food wise. We will grow all the fruit and vegetables needed to feed the children. We intend to keep chickens, ducks, goats and dairy cows.

I am so delighted to say the work started on the 28th of July 2008. To see my vision becoming a reality is fantastic!! I cannot explain all the emotions I am going through.

Not only do we have to build the Happy House, it must also be furnished. Beds, a kitchen, washrooms and toilet facilities, are needed; living quarters for staff; a dining hall that can double as a recreation room. Children need their own space as they grow and their own privacy. We are not going to put these kids in large dormitories; we will have small units; it is a home not an institution. When the house is complete we still have to feed and clothe our children, pay wages and bills.

The three schools already built by the charity will provide a guaranteed quality education. Some of the orphans attending school will become Happy House Kids, as their living conditions at the present time are very unsatisfactory. Some are living with relatives or neighbours who are unable to care for them and their own children. These children already have sponsors through our Sponsored Child Scheme. There is a clinic at school where their medical needs are attended.

The Happy House will thrive with caring, supportive staff and the backing of its sponsors, volunteers and trustees. Without it, these children would be destitute, finding scraps to eat in the bush and sleeping rough. They would have no home, no medicines and no education, no future and the great possibility of not surviving at all.

This project will provide a vital link for so many children, who will pass through its doors over the next 99 years and beyond. Children who will hold their heads high and be proud to say "I was a Happy House Kid".

Work started on the building at the end of August 2008 and it is progressing well due to the support from so many people. We received very generous donations from Nyumbani UK, Coca-Cola Africa, Zurich, Scott Bader and The Jephcott Trust. We need to thank so many people, who have done charity nights in their local pub, sponsored slim and swims, non-uniform days organised by schools and items bought from the Wish List; people who have made donations and who genuinely care about the future of these very defenceless children. You know who you are. Thank you to everyone. It is fantastic what has been achieved for these very defenceless, frightened children. Many who are sleeping rough, begging for food just trying to survive until the Happy House can open its doors to save them from a life of desperation and hopelessness."

20 – RAISING MONEY FOR CHARITY

I am delighted to be associated with this charity. I would thank everyone who has sponsored me. I look forward in 2010 to visiting Watamu with Cherith and see exactly what our efforts have achieved.

Any profit from the sale of this book will go to support the Happy House project.

APPENDICES

Appendix 1

Final Kit List

	WEIGHT (grams)	TOTAL (grams)	GRAND TOTAL (grams)
Rucksack			
Raidlight 30 L	818		
Water bottles	256		
		1074	
Sleeping and Tent Clothes			
Thermarest Prolite 3 Short	427		
Minimus PHD sleeping bag	628		
Tyvek Suit	185		
Skins (leggings)	170		
Merino wool top	241		
Spare socks	52		
Flip flops	183		
		1886	
Compulsory			
Knife (Swiss card)	25		
Topical disinfectant	41		
Anti venom pump (+Gaffer tape)	33		
Whistle (part of bag)			
Compass	29		
Signalling mirror	18		
Survival blanket	46		
Torch and spare batteries	34		
Safety pins	4		
Distress flare	350		
Lighter	23		
		603	
Hygiene			
Soap leaves	14		
Toilet paper	46		
Wet wipes	59		
Tooth brush / paste	14		
P20 (100mls)	111		
Lip balm	8		
Body glide	63		
		315	

APPENDIX 1

Cooking			
Fuel tablets	240		
Tibetan titanium 900 mug	130		
Tibetan titanium tablet stove	10		
Tibetan titanium spork	15		
Windshield	48		
		443	
Medical			
Mycil powder	85		
Zinc oxide tape	34		
Micropore tape	7		
Paracetamol)			
Imodium melts)			
Buccastem)	96		
Ciprofloxacin)			
6 needles)			
Dressings)			
		222	
Food			
Nuun tablets	212		
Day 1	709		
Day 2	674		
Day 3	625		
Day 4	804		
Day 5	635		
Day 6	656		
Day 7	328		
Spare food	525		
Sweets	297		
		5465	
Luxuries			
Garmin charger	16		
Solio charger	177		
Camera and spare battery and card	259		
Note pad / pen	40		
		492	
			10500

Food

	CALORIES	DAILY TOTAL	GRAND TOTAL
DAY 1			
Expedition Muesli	813		
Peperami	126		
Torq Bar	213		
Honey Stinger Bar	180		
Honey Stinger Gel	120		
50G raisins / nuts	188		
Chicken noodle snack	243		
Expedition chicken korma	807		
		2690	
DAY 2			
Expedition porridge with sultanas	806		
Peperami	126		
Honey Stinger Gel	120		
Cliff Bar	240		
Torq Bar	213		
50G raisins / nuts	188		
Creamy cheese pasta	301		
Expedition spaghetti bolognese	806		
		2800	
DAY 3			
Jordan's nut crunch	432		
Skimmed milk	87		
2 peperami	252		
Torq Bar	208		
Honey Stinger Gel	120		
Cliff Bar	240		
Chicken noodle snack	243		
Expedition chicken tikka	808		
50G raisins / nuts	188		
		2578	
DAY 4			
Expedition chilli con carne	807		
2 peperami	252		
2 Honey Stinger Gels	240		
Honey Stinger Bar	190		
Torq Bar	213		
Cliff Bar	250		
100G raisins / nuts	376		
Creamy cheese pasta	301		

APPENDIX 1

100G Jordan's nut crunch	481		
Skimmed milk	87		
		3197	
DAY 5			
90G Jordan's nut crunch	432		
Skimmed milk	87		
2 peperami	252		
Cliff Bar	250		
Honey Stinger Bar	180		
Chicken noodle snack	243		
Expedition spaghetti Bolognese	806		
Expedition rice pudding	264		
		2514	
DAY 6			
90G Jordan's nut crunch	432		
Skimmed milk	87		
Peperami	126		
Honey Stinger Gel	120		
Cliff Bar	256		
Honey Stinger bar	180		
Creamy cheese pasta	301		
50G raisins / nuts	188		
Expedition curried beef and rice	800		
		2490	
DAY 7			
Expedition muesli with milk	813		
Mule Bar	255		
Honey Stinger Gel	120		
		1188	
SPARE BAG			
Expedition custard with berries	592		
Expedition rice pudding	264		
Expedition custard with apple	573		
Mule Bar	270		
Torq Bar	217		
		1916	
36 Nuun Tablets			
Sweets		1090	
			20463

Appendix 2 – TENT 95 Results

RICHARD WEBSTER

STAGE	TIME (Hours, minutes and seconds)	TIME BEHIND FIRST FINISHER (Hours, minutes and seconds)	AVERAGE PACE (Km/hour)	POSITION
First	4.11.17	1.37.12	7.88	170
Second	4.46.49	2.05.32	7.53	166
Third	14.56.39	6.48.17	6.09	152
Fourth	4.39.24	1.47.01	9.06	128
Overall	28.34.09	12.06.43	7.08	135

STEVE CUSHING

STAGE	TIME (Hours, minutes and seconds)	TIME BEHIND FIRST FINISHER (Hours, minutes and seconds)	AVERAGE PACE (Km/hour)	POSITION
First	6.18.15	3.44.10	5.23	676
Second	6.41.57	4.00.40	5.37	616
Third	17.56.36	9.48.14	5.07	362
Fourth	6.58.05	4.05.42	6.06	511
Overall	37.54.53	21.27.27	5.33	449

NICK ZAMBELIS

STAGE	TIME (Hours, minutes and seconds)	TIME BEHIND FIRST FINISHER (Hours, minutes and seconds)	AVERAGE PACE (Km/hour)	POSITION
First	6.24.17	3.50.12	5.15	692
Second	7.49.04	5.07.47	4.60	754
Third	22.27.07	14.18.45	4.05	522
Fourth	9.11.00	6.18.37	4.60	721
Overall	45.51.28	29.24.02	4.41	619

APPENDIX 2

MARTIN HALLWORTH

STAGE	TIME (Hours, minutes and seconds)	TIME BEHIND FIRST FINISHER (Hours, minutes and seconds)	AVERAGE PACE (Km/hour)	POSITION
First	8.10.01	5.35.56	4.04	791
Second	7.49.04	5.07.47	4.60	754
Third	22.27.05	14.18.43	4.05	521
Fourth	9.11.00	6.18.37	4.60	721
Overall	47.37.10	31.09.44	4.25	650

RUSSELL MULDOON

STAGE	TIME (Hours, minutes and seconds)	TIME BEHIND FIRST FINISHER (Hours, minutes and seconds)	AVERAGE PACE (Km/hour)	POSITION
First	6.24.17	3.50.12	5.15	692
Second	8.20.17	5.39.00	4.32	774
Third	27.03.30	18.55.08	3.36	670
Fourth	9.11.00	6.18.37	4.60	721
Overall	50.59.04	34.31.38	3.97	712

ROB JACKSON

STAGE	TIME (Hours, minutes and seconds)	TIME BEHIND FIRST FINISHER (Hours, minutes and seconds)	AVERAGE PACE (Km/hour)	POSITION
First	8.09.56	5.35.51	4.04	789
Second	8.20.17	5.39.00	4.32	774
Third	28.47.45	20.39.23	3.16	716
Fourth	7.14.51	4.22.28	5.82	555
Overall	52.32.49	36.05.23	3.85	735

JOE SKINNER

STAGE	TIME (Hours, minutes and seconds)	TIME BEHIND FIRST FINISHER (Hours, minutes and seconds)	AVERAGE PACE (Km/hour)	POSITION
First	8.09.59	5.35.54	4.04	790
Second	9.05.36	6.24.19	3.96	785
Third	30.00.31	21.52.09	3.03	729
Fourth	10.06.47	7.14.24	4.17	749
Overall	57.22.53	40.55.27	3.52	760

ANT RILEY

STAGE	TIME (Hours, minutes and seconds)	TIME BEHIND FIRST FINISHER (Hours, minutes and seconds)	AVERAGE PACE (Km/hour)	POSITION
First	8.16.16	5.42.11	3.99	800
Second	9.08.48	6.27.31	3.94	790
Third	30.00.31	21.52.09	3.03	749
Fourth	10.06.47	7.14.24	4.17	749
Overall	57.32.22	41.04.56	3.51	761